"Michael captures the raw emotional reality of growing up in an abusive household, where feelings of being helpless and trapped are relentless. Michael's strength and willpower to seek a journey toward light rather than darkness is inspirational. His courage and perseverance to not be afraid of who he is and where he comes from is admirable to the lives that are touched by his story. Michael Doray is my motivational mentor!"

—Elaine Austin, sister

"Michael Doray has captured the soul of self, challenging the safe assumptions about what it means to be fully alive. Taking a moment to get your bearings on what is most important to you, what gets in your way, and finding your courage to be who you were meant to be is what Michael has so deliberately taken the time to write about. He's lived it, and now he shares it with his readers; a worthy read indeed."

—Glen Howard, life coach and mentor

"This book is another remarkable achievement from a young man who has overcome many of life's setbacks through sheer willpower. He has always had a powerful thirst for excellence and the determination to accomplish things he had been told he would never be able to accomplish. Like Michael, may you reach your goals and dreams and help your friends and others do the same!"

—Jim Ward, friend and mentor

FINDING POSITIVITY

A Memoir

MICHAEL DORAY

iUniverse, Inc.
Bloomington

Finding Positivity

Under no circumstances is this book meant to be used as reprisal or to be vindictive. It is meant to capture the experiences and emotions that have transpired in my life and the lessons learned.

iUniverse books may be ordered through booksellers or by contacting:

iUniverse
1663 Liberty Drive
Bloomington, IN 47403
www.iuniverse.com
1-800-Authors (1-800-288-4677)

ISBN: 978-1-4759-1951-6 (sc)
ISBN: 978-1-4759-1953-0 (e)
ISBN: 978-1-4759-1952-3 (dj)

Library of Congress Control Number: 2012908082

Printed in the United States of America

iUniverse rev. date: 6/13/2012

To the Crum family, John, Lisa, Valerie, John-Paul, Kaylene, and Brandan, thank you for all of your love and inspiration.

To my cancer-surviving mom, Karen—thank you for all you've done. You are an inspiration. To my brother, Billy, and sisters, Elaine and Cheryl, thank you for your continued support and love.

A special thanks to all of my close friends, mentors, and coaches along the way.

Contents

FOREWORD

By Brandan Crum, MD

It is of great respect and privilege to have the opportunity to write the foreword for *Finding Positivity*. I have had the true honor of knowing Michael Doray for almost ten years, and his life story has been an impeccable inspiration to me and my journey through life. *Finding Positivity* is written from the many personal experiences Michael shares. He truly demonstrates the willpower of a young man who has overcome an environment of child abuse, heartache, and deprivation. His stories are dynamic and powerful and his experiences are honest and filled with emotion.

As a physician of emergency medicine, I have had many experiences in my life. My journey to becoming a doctor and current career as a physician have been filled with countless mental, physical, emotional, and spiritual challenges. I often think about my journey and the numerous personal sacrifices and struggles I made to get where I am in my life. Although unique in their own context, not one of my struggles or sacrifices can be compared to those of Michael's. For someone who has been through so much, he has accomplished and achieved more than most people I can say I know, including myself. Throughout his hardships existed numerous opportunities to become derailed, lose hope, and just give up. However, by *Finding Positivity*, his will to happily live life to the fullest in all of its aspects prevailed and is surely an inspiration to all, even the strongest at heart.

I have heard and witnessed some of the saddest stories of tragedy, abuse, and death that have brought me to tears. At the same time, I have been given the chance to witness and be a part of some of life's miracles and some of the most happiest and meaningful moments in people's lives. *Finding Positivity* is truly a reflection of these happy and sad life moments. Through his life examples, his book begins through the eyes of an abused child who overcame neglect and sadness and grew to become one of the happiest and most successful people I know today.

Michael's life story has touched me in a unique way. His stories are valuable depictions of personal challenges and successes that remind me that everyone has a story, and no two stories are ever the same. As a physician, I often look for examples of those who have overcome adversity and challenges and stayed the course to be able to take advantage of opportunities to achieve success. To this day, I have yet to discover a personal story of triumph and success quite like that of Michael Doray's.

I applaud Michael for taking the time and effort to produce this motivating memoir on how, if we find positivity in our lives, we can achieve our dreams and overcome our own life challenges. Throughout my life I have learned that success doesn't always happen to the swiftest, the smartest, the strongest, or those with the most advantages. *Finding Positivity* is a true testament to this statement. Anyone reading his book will undoubtedly take away something positive from it. For me, it is an inspiring and humbling reminder of overcoming limited beliefs and never giving up or losing hope. His life story is influential, and I commend and admire Michael for his work and desire to help all of us by sharing his story.

Thank you, Michael, for being that beacon of hope and inspiration to all, especially those with a similar life story as yours, who are looking for the positivity in life that you exemplify so well.

Brandan E. Crum, MD
Emergency Medicine

Introduction

My name is Michael, and I was born in Berkeley, California, in 1981. I am the youngest out of four siblings. My two older sisters are named Elaine and Cheryl, and my older brother is Billy. I grew up in Vallejo.

I sifted and mulled through many of my Vallejo memories for years. I considered publishing this book for years with the hope that my story will help someone else. In recent years of helping others, I realized that my story about finding positivity could help others find their own positivity.

Many of my childhood memories are very painful, difficult, and hard to deal with. I share my own story of overcoming an environment filled with physical and emotional abuse, and the limiting beliefs I faced because of that abuse.

In this book, I explore many doubts, fears, and perplexities from various life situations and demonstrate how I found comfort and self-esteem through volunteering.

I volunteered through most of my early years to a cause that gave me a sense of purpose and solid direction. Volunteering in a nursing home helped guide me through tough years by creating strong relationships with people I looked up to.

Volunteering more than three thousand hours of my adolescent life in a nursing home had a profound impact on my life. Spending those hours in a nursing home was a unique experience that showed me at an early age so much about life.

I am known to be very positive. No matter how bad things get, I always find the positive in life situations. No matter the challenge, I have always looked for a spark of positivity, even when I was so young. Thinking bright, thinking big, thinking greater of myself, I have always seen opportunity in the face of adversity.

The purpose of this memoir is to inspire the uninspired through my personal life story. My greatest wish is that this book inspires, that it instills hope and positivity in others who have gone down tough roads and in people who are looking for ways to be more positive about life.

If you truly wish to be inspired and grasp my concepts of positivity, this book is for you. I choose to share my life in hopes of inspiring others to realize the true strength we all possess inside.

About the Author

When Michael was just twelve years old, he was looking for ways to inspire the uninspired. While volunteering most of his teenage years in a nursing home, Michael found a gift that he could use to help others through his positivity and time spent volunteering. The gift was a way he had of inspiring others by appreciating people for who they were. From early on, he led others by showing people they had the ability to be stronger than they thought they could ever be.

He inspired others and made a difference through countless hours of one-on-one time with patients. In fact, The California Association of Health Facilities in 1995 awarded him Volunteer of the Year award for the whole state of California after he contributed thousands of hours in making a difference.

Michael continued his journalism career by taking part as a sports editor of the Hogan High School newspaper and quickly moved on to become a correspondent for the *Vallejo Times Herald.*

While still in high school, Michael found ways to inspire others while balancing a busy school schedule that included leading a track team and working at McDonald's. McDonald's quickly saw the leadership skills and made him a store manager. Yes, he did newsletters at McDonald's too! From there he moved on to finance and has made banking his main career since 1999.

Among those years, he still used the power of writing as he created newsletters for various teams he led, managed, and inspired. Throughout those years, he has always been a successful performer and has always led successful teams that he managed.

Although the memoirs were an excellent way for Michael to grow personally, they also helped him realize how he can impact others. Michael has built his whole life around inspiring others and helping others overcome limiting beliefs. He loves public motivational speaking and has used this gift several times winning many awards from Toastmasters International.

Michael has overcome many hard times and has faced countless limiting beliefs. He has centered his whole life around positive and inspiring coaches, mentors, friends, and relatives who truly have helped make the difference for him. In this book, he shows the importance of surrounding yourself with positive people.

Michael is currently managing at a large financial institution.

CHAPTER 1
SURVIVING CHILD ABUSE

At the age of five, I was introduced to violence too damn early. Hurt, pain, anger, fear, darkness and despair were all introduced to me too damn early.

My hard family life was at times almost unbearable. Too many times, I worried about how I would pull through. Make another day, tell another lie, then go to God and ask another why.

As a young child and a victim of child abuse, I learned early on about survival, avoidance, and walking on eggshells. I learned how to hide my feelings from others and myself. Drenched in my own state of solitude, ignoring, avoiding, and putting my feelings on the back burner became my sustained routine. Unfortunately, I became great at hiding away my feelings. I hid from my feelings, as if I were hiding from them under a table.

Accounts of Abuse

As a child, I remember being introduced to the gut wrenching pain of seeing my mother being abused. When my father came towards me with his rage, she would intervene, and he would attack her in front of me. While being the youngest child out of four, I saw and heard far too much abuse. Not only did I see my mom suffer, but I saw my brother and two sisters suffer the pains and arduous tragedies of physical and sustained emotional abuse.

The abuse continued for years, leaving scars and the need for lifelong healing processes. The abuse I had seen everyone else go through soon happened to me. Abuse I saw my family go through was harder for me to deal with instead of the actual physical and emotional abuse I suffered.

The abuse became a repetitive nightmare that occurred for years. Sounds of the abuse resounded over and over in my head on countless nights. Abuse flashbacks sifted through my mind, as if I was watching a horrible slide show.

During January 1988, I went through the pain and devastation of witnessing my sister Cheryl get beat up by my father. The sounds of the abuse and screaming I will never forget. I could literally feel my heart racing, beat by beat, moment by moment, tear after tear. It was screaming that ignited and triggered all tragic emotions that no young child should ever have to experience.

The anxious adrenaline and trepidation kicked in like an earthquake shaking me. It hurt so bad to see my sisters go through such abuse. I wanted to do something and could do nothing. I felt powerless. There was nothing in my control, power, or might to do anything other than to grasp and clinch my hands with hope—sheer hope that my father would stop or my sister would get away. I saw that sheer hope slip away too frequently, letting me down every single time.

Days after this attack on my sister, Child Protective Services came to our house. They interviewed everyone separately and took a report of the abuse accounts. But they took no action other than interviews and meaningless talks.

In July 1988, my sister Elaine was seventeen years old and she was beat up so badly that she was literally covered in bruises. She immediately packed her belongings and ran away from home. Elaine ran to her friend's house, which was just blocks away. Elaine was crying, torn down and torn apart with emotions. Mr. Tanner, who was her friend's father, intervened without hesitation. Quickly, he suggested taking Elaine to the police.

Shortly thereafter, Elaine was walking up the twenty-plus stairs of the entrance to the police department. At this moment, she was so scared and fearful. She knew she had to do this for not only herself but for the rest of us. It was for my brother, Billy, my sister, Cheryl, and me. It took her so much courage to do this. After all, she and everyone else were told repeatedly never to tell anyone.

Elaine, being the oldest sister, wanted to do everything she could to turn my father in, knowing everyone else was still in danger and at great risk. We were all so much younger and risked possibilities that were dreadful to imagine.

The Vallejo Police quickly let her in, noticing something terrible had happened. They quickly took a report as the black-and-blue bruises clearly showed. The police wasted no time responding to our Ashton Street address.

The police rang our doorbell, and I immediately knew it was them. My hands were shaking from the drama unfolding. I will never forget the trembling of my hands and the anxious thoughts.

When they came inside the house, I was so scared. Again the adrenaline and heavy heart of emotions resurfaced. I hid in my room and stayed quiet so I could hear everything. I remember shaking and feeling deep pain, knowing what my sister was going through. During the police visit my father admitted to the abuse.

The police sent their report to the district attorney's office and counseling was suggested by the police. My father went to counseling; however, that was short lived.

Due to the fact that my sister made the police report, my father did not want Elaine near the house. She continued to stay with her close friend. When my sister filed the report and photographs were taken, Child

Protective Services never made a follow-up to their initial visit earlier in the year. The police did note the CPS visit.

Years went by as Elaine moved away and my father did not allow her to come see me. Elaine would send birthday and holiday cards, only for my father to intercept them and block our relationship. On December 25, 1988, my father wrote a letter which stated the following:

> Dear Elaine,
> After much thought I find it totally inappropriate to accept any kind of gifts to me or my family from you at this time, especially since the problem has not been resolved. Thank you, Dad.

Graduating high school is perhaps one of the most important days of a person's life. During Elaine's graduation, she went through the pain of graduating without her own family there to cheer her on. Knowing I was not allowed to see my sister graduate was the dismal, sad reality of our family life. It was clear to me that I could never report any abuse as the consequences were too great.

My father even blocked our grandparents on my mother's side from being a part of our lives during the final years of their own lives. Having the special bond with our grandparents cut short was tragic and devastating.

During this time, massive tension headaches began to take hold of my life. I started getting these headaches

5

weekly during third grade. They prevented me from focusing in school. The headaches became so severe that I would only want to put my head on a pillow, in a dark room, and sleep. The tension would continuously build up, forcing me to throw up every time I experienced the headaches.

My grades in school were just good enough to get by, and I started to isolate myself from friends. Family troubles were made evident in my schoolwork. The signs of abuse showed in my negative and struggling school performance. I came across my first-grade report card. My teacher, Ms. Bogart, cited the following on March 3, 1988:

> Michael does not communicate his needs or wants. He has never initiated a conversation with me. He tends to be very dreamy. His name is put on a list as possible retention. Parents and I need to be in closer contact.

One of the most serious incidents of abuse occurred when I was just in third grade. The bruises on my face were so bad that I could not go to school for three weeks. The bruises were tough to look at every day in the mirror. Chicken pox was the excuse given to the school as to why I was gone for those three weeks.

It was Christmastime, and I will never forget the Christmas card my class made for me. It still touches me today when I think about how special the card made me feel. When the entire class went through the trouble of making the card and signing it, they never would know how much of a positive impact it made for me.

Ms. Alm, who was my teacher, became suspicious after I was gone for so much time. When I eventually came back to school, the bruises slightly showed. I was so frightened because school pictures were just around the corner. Upon arriving at class, Ms. Alm took me aside and looked into my eyes. She asked me repeatedly, "What happened to you? Are you okay?"

She came right out and asked the infamous question, using the word I never considered—or, frankly, never even knew what it really meant. She said, "Michael, are you being abused? Why do you have bruises?" I told her I had fallen over my cat and everything was fine. Ms. Alm looked at me with disbelief and concern and I remember hearing the thumping of my heart during that uncomfortable talk.

While being tipped off by Ms. Alm, our school principal became suspicious of physical abuse. The principal spoke to my father on a few occasions. After all, he did know my father; the principal had been our next-door neighbor for some time.

I had every opportunity to tell people but pretended everything was fine. I simply could not muster the courage to tell anyone.

The Speech Therapist

Teachers continued to worry about my slow progress and referred me to a speech therapist on campus. I could never forget the name of the therapist. Her name was Ms. Reed, and I would see her every Wednesday afternoon.

I remember walking up the stairs to the trailer that Ms. Reed was in. The trailer was in the middle of campus, right next to the play yard. The fear I felt every time I went to see her was enormous. I was so scared that she would find out about the abuse in some way or another.

She would put flash cards in front of me to quiz my ability to name off what was on the cards. We did therapy exercises together for months. I did note to myself that only kids with problems would go see Ms. Reed. So I felt that I was one of those singled-out kids. Although I knew Ms. Reed was there to help, I knew I was smarter than I let others believe.

I often took shelter in my own dark caves of thoughts and deep canyons of loneliness. Since I was so scared, I stayed pretty quiet, and Ms. Reed was deeply concerned about my progress. Ms. Reed suggested to my parents additional tutoring and strong counseling. The school was mystified at what was holding me back from being a performing student.

The Counselor

The counselor was supposed to uncover my problem. Every Tuesday after school for several months my father would drive me to see the counselor in downtown Vallejo. I was so terrified to talk with the counselor. My palms would clam up and my headaches would kick in like the intensity of a passing freight train. I wondered what lies I would tell, which stories I would assemble and scramble together.

The counselor kindly offered me pecan cookies and had me sit in a comfy yellow chair during every visit. I have a sweet tooth and loved those cookies! The comfortable atmosphere was not nourishing enough for me to have the ability to tell. Nor did it provide for me the comfort of knowing everything would be secret if I was truthful. I didn't feel safe.

I was feeling so discouraged, lonely, and sad. My spirit was dejected. My center focus was showing that everything was fine at home.

We had conversations that really didn't go anywhere since I stayed in my shell. He had a talent for juggling, and he did this to trigger a laugh. There was some positive that did come about with this counselor. He did give me someone to talk to about school, and he did build rapport with me. At least he tried to. Yet he was never able to uncover the physical and emotional abuse that I was suffering at home. Every visit left me feeling so lonely, empty and isolated.

The Family Doctor

Next I was referred to my primary care doctor since my headaches did not go away and were oftentimes extremely severe. At one point, Dr. Nelson, who was our family doctor, began to wonder if stress was triggering my tension headaches.

Dr. Nelson started to ask my parents deeper questions about my home life. After his brilliant possible findings and emerging curiosity, his suspicion grew. My father told Dr. Nelson that stress could not be a factor. I distinctly remember my father telling him that the junipers outside the house were causing the flares of headaches. After that visit, I remember my father telling my mom what a horrible doctor he was for trying to blame the headaches on tension and stress. I was never taken back to see Dr. Nelson ever again.

The Catholic Nun

Soon I was introduced to a nun at the St. Vincent's Catholic Church in Vallejo. The nun became my personal tutor. I began seeing her twice a week after school. One of my parents would drop me off every Tuesday and Thursday at 3:30 p.m., and I remained there until 5:30 p.m.

During those long two hours that the nun worked with me, I never paid attention. All I could focus on was how slowly the clock was going. She would have me practice multiple-choice questions to test how well I was doing. I remember going step-by-step through math equations.

During that time, I just pretended I was listening and following her. Pretending is what I became great at doing. I practiced daily how to pretend.

When it came time for me to take a test with her, I would just guess, as I really didn't care. I simply didn't have the desire and motivation to do well in school. My brainpower was preoccupied worrying about my safety and the safety of my family.

Any schoolwork that required me to really focus became damn near impossible. For example, remembering what I was reading and figuring out math equations were some of my biggest struggles. My critical thinking skills were used up in critically thinking about being beaten up. I simply could not focus. I could not do it, no matter how hard I was trying. I was only thinking about being picked up and taken to the place that I dreaded the most.

The thoughts of going home haunted me. All I could think about were the painful flashbacks of yelling and abuse. I was so worried about getting in the car with my dad that I would almost pee my pants every single time. This was because he had beaten me up in the car once after a movie he took my brother and me to see. The entire car ride home consisted of backhand blows to my face, yelling and cursing. At every red light, he would backhand me. He threatened me that when we got home he would smash my head through a glass door. This threat stuck with me forever and I never could forget how helpless I was.

From that point on, being alone with my father in a car scared the living daylights out of me every single time. The anxiety I felt anytime I had to get in the car with my father from that point on was terrifying.

Abuse continued for years. Years of seeing the ones I loved the most getting beaten began to take a toll on me emotionally.

My father isolated my mom in her own separate room. For five long years, I watched my mom cry as she suffered and felt helpless. This was her punishment because my father was insecure of my relationship with her. Our house felt like a prison and seemed to have been managed like a prison.

There were consequences if anyone flushed a toilet while my father was in the shower. Consequences, if anyone ever accidentally awoke my father from sleep. We were not allowed to ever clear our throats near our father. We risked consequences if we didn't smile right in our school photos. I knew fear all too well.

The physical and emotional abuse prevented me from trusting anyone who tried to help. That door was closed, and I intended to keep it shut to everyone. Fear managed me completely. I will never forget the fear and helplessness that I felt.

During this time, I was not a popular kid in school, which created even more adversity. Many of my classmates would tease me, and the violence at home continued.

Black eyes, bruises and marks, happened too frequently. Fear was my reality. I will never forget the dismal images and the cover-up stories as to why I had bruises. If anything, I became great at telling lies to people who were trying to figure me out.

One day my father literally picked me up by my shirt collars, pressed me up against the wall, and over and over again backhanded my face. After these moments, I wanted to run away so badly but had nowhere to go.

When others would try to help, I never opened the doors for a reason. I didn't feel worthy of help. Fear coursed through my mind during many sleepless nights as I blamed myself and kept asking myself one question: "Why?"

Others didn't seem to be going through what I was going through. This made it confusing for me. It repeatedly presented me the question: "Why is this happening to only my family?"

My mom did take me to Catholic Church consistently. I didn't have much understanding of faith at the time; however, I do remember that I had a cross hanging in my bedroom. I often stared at that cross and would sometimes talk to it. Often I would say, "God, tell me why I deserve this."

I always looked to that cross. In some moments, I had spite over it while wondering why God put me in the situations I was in. That seemed like a very fair question to me. Yet I would look at it and also see the cross as a symbol of hope in my life. All other families seemed normal on the surface. I questioned myself and my own self-worth too many times.

Not once did I experience a happy family vacation. Not once. On every vacation, my father either beat up someone or verbally abused someone. Everyone walked on eggshells in order to try to keep the peace. Eggshells were broken constantly because no matter how perfect everyone was, something small would always go wrong.

Show-and-Tell

Classmates eagerly came back to school after a long summer vacation to show and tell their exciting family travels. They would talk about the cool camping trips, trips to Hawaii, and exciting family excursions. I actually had anxiety about going back to school because I knew that everyone came back with awesome stories. The first thing people would do was talk about what they did.

I asked myself repeatedly, "What did I do?" I did nothing other than hide from my father. I would lie to the class about my trips so I could fit in and be normal. I had no fun stories to tell. Standing in front of all my classmates and lying during show-and-tell was so tragic. After all, I had to get up in front of the class and share something, regardless. I certainly was not going to talk about the awful abuse I had gone through.

In order to be just like everyone else, I manufactured a lovely story. The story was of blue skies, sunshine, and rainbows. Yet on the inside, I felt sadness that consisted of dark skies, clouds and whispers of unworthiness. I wished I could be just like them. I wanted to be popular and was trying desperately to fit in.

I thanked the Lord every time I made it through show-and-tell. From that point on, any time I had to speak in front of others, I would have heavy weights of anxiety on my shoulders.

While growing up, my brother and I had rooms directly across from one another. Anytime my parents would yell, or my father was beating someone, we stood at the front of our doors. We looked at each other with outright fear and justifiable devastation. We both did not know what to do but always wished we had the ability to do something.

A mother's bond with a boy child, I have come to find out, is unique and special in its own graceful way. Boys tend to be very protective of their mothers. Mothers tend to be very protective of their boys. My brother and I were definitely protective. I think this is why it was so difficult for us to see our mom being victimized as she tried to keep the peace.

To stay busy, I tried to have an outlet through soccer, Ninja Turtles, and ThunderCats action heroes. My mom would show up at games and everyone would always wonder where my dad was.

My father never made a game. At almost every soccer game, I saw all of the dads cheering for their kids. Not seeing my dad there made me feel that I was really unworthy of an outgoing dad.

I struggled through some deep feelings of anger, which transformed into pain and even hatred. That deep pain led me to think of suicide far too often when I was eight years old. The thoughts would surface after some tough beatings. Sorting out these thoughts alone was overwhelming. The strong bond with my mom kept me going. So many nights and too many nights, I would lay awake and cry as I fell asleep to the sounds of arguing. I could hear the arguing travel through the walls as if the walls were not even there.

There were so many nights throughout my childhood when I was pulled out of bed and beaten for the smallest of reasons. So many nights I would fall asleep to the voices of yelling, violence, and banging. Too many nights were like this. Too many violent attacks on my loved ones and me were seared into my heart.

I worried often for my brother, sisters, and mom every time someone did something wrong. Since I didn't know of anyone who might be going through the same things, I continued to believe it was just our family. It was also just our bad luck.

During this time, I didn't feel I mattered. I continued to feel like the abuse I went through was perhaps my fault in every situation that came about. I would oftentimes stay awake and talk to myself about how I should have done things differently. Maybe I could have said something a different way or remembered to say something I should have said. Constantly after every argument, or every beating, all night long, these were the questions I asked myself—over and over again.

In spite of it all, I felt resiliency and hope deep in my heart. No matter how bad things were, for some reason I always had the ability to be positive. I always had that unwavering ability to find that positivity is miraculous. But I needed more than positivity to get through. I needed courage, love, strength and needed to be brave. Time was ticking. After all, I was failing in school and just on God's grace was getting by.

In my elementary years, I fortunately was never held back. I squeezed by every year by the skin of my teeth.

During these years of daunting violence and struggles, my older brother and two sisters dealt with things in their own ways. I learned to cope on my own. We all coped silently in our own internal landscapes, which were covered with busy highways. They were highways that led us to difficult junctions; bumpy, graveled side routes; and at times densely foggy paths.

I hoped for a better life and vowed to myself I would grow up fast so I could have a better life faster. My positivity kept me going, my faith kept me alive, and I began to tightly clench on to my internal will for a better life.

CHAPTER 2
PURPOSE, POSITIVITY, AND VOLUNTEERING

Finding My Purpose

To escape the abuse, I begged my mom to take me to her work. I wanted to stay as far away from home as possible. Without hesitation, my mom agreed. She was a nurse at a Convalescent hospital, a long-term care facility in Vallejo.

I was just eight years old when I experienced the life of a nursing home. Although being with my mom as much as possible wouldn't allow me to avoid the abuse completely, it at least minimized it—a bit.

While I was at my mom's work, I began doing little tasks that were helpful. For example, I would clean the birdcage constantly. The administrative assistants had me deliver messages and packages to various departments.

In time, people at my mom's work began to appreciate the smallest of deeds. They would always comment on my smile. Soon, they recognized me for making a difference.

After some time, I increased the number of tasks around the facility. For the first time in my life, I began to feel that I mattered! People could count on me. I began to feel a sense of purpose!

While getting older, the hospital administrator suggested that I apply to become a volunteer. I was eager to get started. The day was April 1, 1994, and I was so excited to fill out a volunteer application! After all, I was pretty upset that there were laws that prohibited adolescents my age from working. If I could have worked legally at age ten, I would have done it! Volunteering was my only legal option.

When I turned twelve, many people still believed I was too young to assist patients living in a nursing home. I continued to fill out my official volunteer application.

I truly believe no one is ever too young or too old to volunteer. As long as you are breathing, you have the ability to inspire, help others, and make a difference for other human beings. Why put an age on that?

I was available on all weekends and every single day after school. There was a question on the application that asked, "What qualities do you possess that you feel would make you a good volunteer?" I wrote, "I like to draw, make things, help patients hang things up, and read to them."

I signed the application and turned it in to the activity director, Ellie. She saw that I was passionate about helping. Quickly she accepted my application, and this became a positive experience that would help shape my adolescent years. I worked with Ellie for years to come.

I became a friend to many of the patients in the nursing home. I started to run bingo games, direct trivia sessions, and help the activity department prepare for entertainment events. I read out loud to patients who were paralyzed and helped patients make phone calls to loved ones. I pushed patients in their wheelchairs from one side of the facility to another. Some patients would just sit in their wheelchairs in the same spots, so I would move them in front of windows or near a radio. The patients loved to be rolled to the patio area outside so they could soak up a few minutes of sun. Moving them around sure made a difference. Maybe this was a small difference, but the smallest differences can really be the biggest differences!

After every volunteer shift, my mom and I would drive home and during the drive, I reflected. A sense of peace, happiness, and belonging settled within me.

A teenager volunteering in a nursing home was certainly not the popular or trendy thing to do. But for me, helping others just seemed to be the right thing to do. I found my gift for helping people and being positive truly made a difference in many lives.

Volunteering became a calling for me.

Although I was flourishing as a volunteer, my family life was still a challenge. I started to be proactive with my mindset and knew my future depended on it. I needed to make the most of the moments I was in. I needed to survive. Not survival in the sense I would die but survival in the sense I needed to go in the right direction in life. I realized that life is tough. It is super tough. The only way to make it through is to know who we really are and to work really, really hard. We have to push ourselves, and when we think we can't push ourselves any harder, that's when we have to push harder.

I was able to see that other people had many of their own struggles. Life was not easy for anyone. Every person has his or her own unique story. Volunteering helped me come to this realization. It helped show me the big picture, that life is all about helping others. We help ourselves by helping others.

We all go through immense challenges, dark times, and tragic moments. No matter how dismal those events may be, we are still responsible for where we end up in life.

For me, survival meant that I wouldn't deviate toward unhealthy lifestyles, such as drugs, wrong friends, and harming myself with depressing thoughts. And I still avoided being at home at all costs. Volunteering helped keep me on this path.

From the earliest days I can remember, faith played a pivotal role in my life. Every Sunday morning, my mom and I would go to the 7:30 Catholic Mass.

After becoming an altar boy, I again felt that nourishing sense of purpose. Church was peaceful, and it fueled my strength, ignited hope, and fired up my soul with belief.

After church on those early Sundays, my mom and I would drive around in order not to go straight home. It was sad that my mom and I actually feared going back home. We dreaded it because it was not a place that gave us happiness. It gave us fears. We continued to drive around until it was time for my piano lessons in a very small, quaint town called Crockett, which was home to a major sugar refinery. Crockett was an old town full of winding hills. It had old train tracks, mom-and-pop businesses, and narrow streets. It was a unique little town that sat on the cool, breezy bay.

During the piano lessons, my mom would read a book downstairs and listen to me plink away on the piano as she waited for the practice to be over.

I was excited to learn how to play the piano so I could play for the patients. Piano lessons were fun, and I maximized every lesson, which helped me to write my own music notes.

Ellie would write "Piano with Michael" on the patient calendar once a week. Patients would be rolled into the large front room called the day room. They sat in front of the piano, and they loved the experience! As I played, patients would just listen. Regardless of a patient's disabilities or conditions, the soothing sounds of the piano provided comfort.

Every music hour made a difference for each of them as they hummed to the familiar old-school tunes. I realized I was making patients happy even if it was for a short while. Seeing the smiles and realizing the difference I was making made me realize my purpose in life.

It was to inspire the uninspired!

To this day, I believe that my purpose in life is to do just that!

Those sad, tired, lonely faces in the nursing home counted on my smiles every single day. I started to develop a new perspective on life simply by getting others to smile. I wanted to make these patients feel that they mattered! After all, they made me feel that I mattered!

My grades in school were getting better as I was more motivated to do well. Headaches began to go away, and my self-confidence grew. I chose to excel in one thing: helping others!

Finding Positive People

I truly started to look up to many of the seniors in the nursing home as mentors. Never will I forget one senior in particular: Ms. Riley. I saw her every visit. She would always look into my eyes and let me know how proud of me she was. For her, I tried to make things positive all the time. Even though she had a lonely life, with no family visitors, she still would always smile. She still stayed positive all of the time. She found the good in every life situation.

Nursing homes can give one a sense of sadness just thinking about them. Typically, a lot of families don't visit their loved ones as often as they could. The nursing home can be sad for a variety of reasons. Often, it is a patient's final home.

I realized when I said my final good-bye just before Ms. Riley died, how much of an impact she really made in my life. People who are naturally positive tend to gravitate toward each other. I realized how lucky I was to have known Ms. Riley. Looking up to positive people can help shape our paths, our lives, who we are and who we were meant to be. If we continue to gravitate toward positive people, we can become more positive.

I learned that we should center ourselves with others who validate our joy. Ms. Riley did validate my joy! When she passed, I saw my seventh-grade picture near her bedside. I realized then that volunteering was about more than making a difference. It was about making an invaluable experience during every visit. She didn't have any pictures of her own kids or grandkids. Ms. Riley didn't have much family. It was just my picture. She in many ways was a grandmother figure for me. I could not remember any memories of my own grandmother and so Ms. Riley sure made that special impact on me. The gift of my time really made the difference for Ms. Riley on her final days.

Making a Difference

During my volunteer time, I documented everything I did and saved the activity logs. They are fun to look at every now and then. Day by day, I wrote down how many room visits I made and what games I played.

Here is a sample of what I wrote:

Thursday, February 20, 1995
—Set up for patient's birthday party, cleaned up party. Took patients on their afternoon cigarette break, did six room visits, handed patients their mail, and helped them read it.

Tuesday, June 10, 1995
—Typed patient council minutes, did nine room visits, set up for bingo, and helped patients play. Worked on the newsletter and got the birthday list together.

Thursday June 12, 1995
—Set up for exercise class. Did twelve room visits, turned on a relaxing film for low-functioning patients, rounded up patients for Catholic communion, and made a voting box for patients.

From stuffing Christmas stockings, wrapping Christmas gifts, and decorating to helping patients color Easter eggs, preparing for holidays meant a lot to the patients.

I created a newsletter for the nursing home and would always recognize birthdays and special occasions. Patients loved the stories in the newsletters. It was amazing to know something as small as a newsletter truly did go a long way toward making others feel appreciated.

Who could ever forget the cigarette breaks? I would wheel some of the patients to the outside patio area and watch them smoke cigarettes. One patient in particular always had to have his Dr. Pepper during the cigarette break. During those times, we would strike up great conversations about life. When I had nothing to say, just the simple fact that I was present created a sense of company, which I knew they valued. The cigarettes gave them a sense of great comfort, even though they were toxic. Cigarettes were all they had to look forward to.

One patient in particular, whom I will never forget, was Ms. Jackson. Ms. Jackson would always wheel herself around the facility, and she loved to crochet. She would participate in every activity event and help me prepare. She would always say to me, "I appreciate everything you are doing for everyone here."

I realized that she counted on me so much for the smallest deeds.

I read to the patients who were comatose and to patients who could do nothing other than clamp on to my hand. The power of giving your time is true power!

27

The power of time I gave became the greatest gift I could give to another. More profoundly, it was the greatest gift I could give to myself. I felt that I was exactly where I was supposed to be when a patient grabbed my hand and I saw a teardrop stream from their eye.

To this day, I take those memories and gifts with me. I learned that I can overcome anything by having an overwhelming force of good.

During this whole time, Ellie kept encouraging me. She believed in me and never realized how much volunteering was actually transforming my own life.

Ellie was just one of many who inspired me to continue on the path of volunteerism. Ellie, the staff, and the patients of the nursing home helped me to cultivate a new beginning. A brighter tomorrow and a path that led me forward. They showed alternatives; they showed me love. They helped me learn who I was and what I was here to do.

Some of the patients began to know of the abuse that I was under, and I would tell some of them whom I felt a connection to. I told them because I knew it was safe. I sought out advice from a few patients.

The best advice I received was from a patient telling me that I was loved and to stay strong. The same patient told me he was always there for me.

During one conversation, Ellie asked, "Are you sure you don't want to be with your friends for the summer?"

I told her, "I am with my friends."

She saw my passion and was amazed that I would sacrifice my time with friends for volunteering. Little did Ellie know that the patients were truly my friends and I'd rather be there volunteering than anywhere else in the world.

Volunteering became a healthy alternative instead of danger that would have been so easy for me to get involved with. Many of my school peers started doing drugs and I steered far away, as I saw the damage and heartbreak it caused far too many people near me. At this moment, I realized that through adversity we do have choices and options.

When the unfriendly monsters of adversity start knocking on our doors of temptations, it is in this time that we have to choose wisely and dig deep into our faith—and I mean *deep*. If we don't, our very lives can be harvested with self-destruction, relentless pain, and sorrow.

In the circumstances of my childhood, as I faced major limiting beliefs, I truly found that inner belief when I dug into my faith and was careful of the doors I opened. I saw too many loved ones open the wrong doors. My faith became my compass. When I was unsure, it would guide me to the right direction. While I was in the worst down times and felt my tank was on empty, out of nowhere that inner belief gave fuel just before I stalled out.

By March 1995, I had logged close to one thousand volunteer hours in the nursing home. This helped me win the Teen Volunteer of the Year award for the state of California. The award was presented by the California Association of Health Facilities (CAHF) on July 10, 1995. I was fourteen years old. Winning gave me a huge boost in confidence, and I have always been incredibly humbled by the award. I realized there are many other volunteers out there.

This was a major accomplishment because it was the first award I won. It was also the first time I flew in an airplane, as my mom and I were flown to San Diego to accept the award.

I continued to volunteer until 1998, which put me at more than three thousand hours of total volunteer time. By then, I was finally old enough to be hired. My first paid job became the assistant activity director.

I am so grateful that during that time I could hear so many incredible stories and meet so many incredible people. It gave me a huge sense of respect for all volunteers who give their time, dedication, and hearts. In life, I am not sure if there is anything more awesome than a volunteer. I experienced how awesome volunteers were as they were always there in times of need for me. If we want to learn who we are, volunteering can show us all.

Cancer Struggles

Years passed by, and my parents divorced. A few years after the divorce, my mom was diagnosed with cancer. During my mom's fight with cancer, it was incredibly painful to see my own mom deteriorate week over week going through chemotherapy.

While seeing my mom go from a healthy state to a declining state, I struggled to find strength of my own. I knew I had to be there for her emotionally. I had to encourage her, stay positive, and continuously be there to listen and offer comfort.

There is no instruction manual a person reads before he or she goes through these hard life events. It would be nice if there was. When we do look around, we realize how much support we really do have.

It is amazing how the smallest deeds others do during a time of great need make all the difference. Life throws challenges our way that we never thought we would experience. When we do experience them, it really opens our eyes to how precious life really is.

While working full time and sharing with my family the responsibility of driving our mom to more than 150 doctor appointments, the pressure ignited a great deal of pain. I found a resource though: The American Cancer Society. One day I picked up the phone and, lo and behold, it was a volunteer!

I called to get advice. Never did I know this phone call would make such an impact. The volunteer who answered shared with me that she was a cancer survivor herself. She told me that she had no kids. She said, "It is so awesome that you are there for your mom. Just your being there for her means more than you will ever know. I don't have any kids, but I would have loved to have kids there just holding my hand. Your mom is lucky to have you all. She needs you all."

My emotions poured out during this phone call. The volunteer just listened and reaffirmed that she was always there for me to call. This is what volunteers do!

As painful as it was to see my mom go through the process, her strength was astonishing and amazed me. She was in the fight of her life. There were battles in the process, and at times it was justifiably overwhelming.

My mom made a remarkable recovery! I saw her face limiting beliefs constantly, and she battled for her life. By sheer perseverance, will, and courage, she beat cancer.

While my mom was in the state she was in, I saw volunteers helping patients and families, and I smiled! The volunteers did all the small things for us that made a difference in a time of anxiety and pain. They asked us if we needed anything as we waited. They told jokes and made us laugh. They offered comfort. This is what volunteers do!

I was amazed at how much volunteers helped me after the whole process was over, not only from the support standpoint at Stanford but by the phone when I really needed them. In a hospital, perhaps the most important position is a volunteer. A volunteer makes everything okay.

Amazing Volunteers

Volunteers are also doing other amazing things. I consider one named John to be my brother. John volunteered in Reno with the Trauma Intervention Center as well as the suicide hotline. He showed up at countless accident scenes at all hours in the night to lend a shoulder to a stranger.

John is there at a person's toughest time and most challenging time to offer a listening ear, a pat on the shoulder, or a simple hug. He offers resources and invaluable time.

I can only imagine how many lives he has saved by volunteering for the suicide hotline. Never did he make a dollar for his time. He did, however, get paid something more than monetary value. He got paid knowing he made a difference. That feeling is priceless.

He gets paid when he closes his eyes at night and knows he could have very well saved a life. He could have saved a family from grief or even a community from grief.

It says a lot about a person who cares about someone he doesn't know. Truly, it shows the greatness in our human spirit when a person puts his own needs aside for the needs of others.

John remains an advocate for suicide prevention and is dedicating his life to helping people. John has likely helped more people than he will ever realize.

This again is what volunteers do all of the time!

Volunteers always seem to be there when we need them the most! No matter the situation. They are there at the suicide lines, child-abuse lines, cancer lines, hospitals, trauma interventions at accident scenes, churches, schools, and everywhere we look. Volunteers are everywhere. This is true when we think about the volunteers of 9/11. It was amazing to see so many people step up and volunteer, risking everything to try to save a life and help.

We continuously see entire communities step up and volunteer, helping each other rebuild after devastating natural events like Hurricane Katrina, massive floods, and tornadoes. The human spirit is a giving spirit. It is always amazing to see. People volunteer continuously because it is the right thing to do. They volunteer by going on field trips with their kids' classes as well as giving their time at homeless shelters and countless nonprofit groups and organizations.

Seeing the power of my own volunteer work really helped show me how awesome it is to volunteer for others. Volunteering taught me perhaps the most valuable lessons of all time: to help in times of need. When we do this, we become more of who we are supposed to be and should be.

Volunteering can give us all a sense of purpose that ignites a light in us. It lit a light for me that ignited into a calling of helping and inspiring others.

Sometimes, we are called to grow up faster than originally planned. However, I believe I was meant to grow up faster than many. Volunteering and getting the satisfaction of knowing I made the difference for many helped me grow up faster than I realized. As I look back on missed opportunities from the home life, like happy family memories and the thought of living in a violence-free home, things that I had no control over happened.

The devastation that I went through was never my fault. I realize that now. Realizing this has given me a huge sense of relief and comfort and has been a key role in my healing process. Through the pain, yes, I realize that through volunteering I was where I was supposed to be. I found my calling in life and from that emerged stronger!

Looking back at all of the experiences I went through with giving my time, I can clearly see how volunteering in a nursing home transformed my life! It helped make my life! Volunteering shows us positivity because volunteering is positivity.

CHAPTER 3
KEEP GOING

As my senior year in high school was approaching, my English teacher convinced me to join a track team. In doing so, I helped create the school's first cross-country team in several years. I was able to convince the same teacher to coach this team.

I began to condition daily after school, working very hard to train to be the best I could be in running. Running became a great outlet and kept me busy. Soon, I was competing against other incredibly determined runners who would brave the long cross-country runs, no matter the weather, no matter the conditions.

Competition Day

The sun was glazing down on a lazy, hot, and muggy Tuesday afternoon. It was a hilly and muddy green park in Vallejo. Fresh-cut, watered-down grass scented the air.

Tall beautiful trees covered the park, leaving glimpses of cool, protective shade. Sprinklers had just turned off, which left huge mud holes hidden under heaps of leaves. These hazards, along with the saturated soil, were the perfect ingredients for creating a treacherous and brutal three-mile cross-country trail.

Competitive athletes ended their stretching and lined up for the start of the long race. Moments before the gunshot fired off, I looked around and saw determined athletes. They all had a great deal of pride in their eyes.

I had prepared myself for this thirty-two-hundred-meter event with months of relentless conditioning. Hours and days of exhausting practice and mental mind building would finally be tested.

Facing Limiting Beliefs

Throughout the day prior to the event, I felt a huge sensation of stress. I knew that I was competing against sharp talent. The stress of competing in general always meddles with one's personal strength, pride, and will. That day, I knew upon watching the spectators, I wanted to win. Most of all, I knew within myself that I was capable of it.

While growing up under a roof of overwhelming challenges, running was a significant outlet. Aiming to win and being great in it were as important as ever to me.

When we want something badly enough, our personal strength in our depths can be amazing, as we discover strengths that we never knew we had. Although I was determined as I was preparing for the race, a feeling of limiting belief clouded my mind. The gunshot echoed in the air. The sound triggered a powerful surge in my foot as I felt my shoe press against the slippery mud. With a surge of force, I took off on the long event.

There was naturally an intensity of fear among many of the athletes as there always is before any sporting event. I felt that fear for sure. Overcoming that fear and sticky sensation of limiting belief would be important for me during this race. Not overcoming this could prevent my victory. Unequivocal doubt and stomach acid ran through my veins. Pressure and stress kept throwing fragments of limiting beliefs my way.

Suddenly, I started to impress myself as I noticed my huge personal progress! I started to pass one runner at a time. Out of nowhere, I gained my personal mojo!

A strong push of inner belief fueled my energy. An invigorating, brisk, fresh wind glided through the back of my shirt. Suddenly, I was in second place! Within moments, I was looking at the back of my competitor's head. He was always so easy to remember. After all, he had a long, blond ponytail and huge calf muscles. The ponytail would always annoy me because I had looked at it in many prior races. Too many prior races! This race was my race!

He had always beaten me while competing in track relays. For the longest time, I had wanted to claim victory over him. This thought fueled my motivation and sharpened my competitiveness to win.

Coach Lapid screamed at the top of her lungs, "You are so close! You are doing it, Mike!"

Soon, I was right behind my competitor, almost within an arm's distance. I initiated my strong and final kick slightly before he did. I surged past him, which brought me to first place!

I did not pay attention to any detail other than winning. I could not hear anything other than the intensity of my own breathing and my running shoes slamming against the trail. My cheeks and body temperature were as hot as a stove. I was just focusing on the finish line, and everything around me was a blur.

I won the thirty-two-hundred-meter with a time of 11:56. This was my fastest three-mile victory and my new personal best. The refreshing taste of victory showed me that I can do something if I want it badly enough!

The self-created limiting beliefs we impose on ourselves are amazing. They can hold us hostage from taking control of our dreams. They can hold us back from living the life we were meant to live.

We can push aside limiting beliefs when we choose to push them aside. We do have the power to prove those thoughts wrong. The power to step out of comfort zones and claim many personal victories is always within us. We cannot claim victories without stepping outside our comfort zones. I surely was testing my comfort zones while I was competing in cross-country and track.

Everyone experiences these similar limiting beliefs at some point or another. When we do experience them and prove them wrong, our confidence levels help us weather other personal life challenges. The same feeling I experienced with a limiting belief in competing is similar to what we all experience in everyday life. Literally!

The truth is that every day of our lives we are seeking our own real potential. In many cases, others around us try to push us to it. Coach Lapid tried to do that for me. However, one thing always seemed to stand in the way: my own limiting beliefs.

Self-imposed limiting beliefs tend to be the traffic that slows us down on our internal highway. When we dig deeply enough in ourselves, that discovery can be monumental. As we discover this stupendous power, we become inspired within ourselves.

Perseverance was the key ingredient that helped me sustain the ability to win my race. I had a goal to win, stuck with it, and didn't give up. The will to win when we want something badly enough is incredible!

Public Speaking

People push themselves, sometimes to the farthest of limits, to outwit their limiting beliefs. Some people drive themselves constantly to take risks. For example, lots of people hate public speaking, and some literally have phobias over it. When I started my banking career, I learned of a public speaking network called Toastmasters.

Toastmasters is a public-speaking forum that helps professionals build public-speaking skills. While I was joining the organization, I had a slight, fickle disposition hovering over me. I was unsure if this was what I really wanted to do. The awful childhood memories of speaking in front of others continued to give me anxiety with public speaking.

I signed up and took a risk. Somewhere deep inside me, I wondered if this possible talent existed. Once I started to attend the meetings and gave some speeches for the very first time, I remember the gut-wrenching thoughts. The deep echoes of limiting beliefs caved in.

Limiting beliefs would make me second-guess myself with thoughts grumbling like this: "Not sure if I can do this. I may not be good enough. Am I really worthy of winning since other people are so good?"

What I discovered was it is okay to get out of my comfort zone and take a risk. *After all,* I thought, *the worst thing that can happen is I could utterly embarrass myself and fail at giving a speech.*

I actually did pretty well in all of the speeches. My success in public speaking started to blast off! I gained a new confidence.

What a big surprise: I was doing better than I ever thought I could do. I began to feel a sense of glory—just like feeling the glory of winning in a race! I became thrilled at giving speeches.

It didn't take long, after doing speeches every week, for me to start competing. After presenting a competing speech and winning, I won a huge award. This was a big deal for me. Winning the speech gave me the green light to compete in the 2001 San Francisco/Western Region Finals.

Out of nowhere, I was spending several weeks preparing for a huge speech. During the speech preparations, they notified us that this speech would be bigger than originally thought, as hundreds of people would watch.

The day of the speech came quickly: November 8, 2001. I started making the drive to San Francisco, and the nerves were running through my body. My mom and sister Elaine were in the car with me.

This was a great opportunity for me to truly showcase my talent. Upon arriving at the building where the speeches were, I found that my hands were shaking vigorously. My nerves rattled like a rattlesnake prepping for attack. The competitor in me wanted to earn nothing less than first place.

I received a tour of the huge PG&E auditorium, and guests were starting to arrive. Top executives were showing up. My bosses and even a college professor entered the auditorium. The pressure was on!

In the staging area, as I was standing with my peers, the speeches began. We all listened to the other participants. We heard a few candidates stumble through.

My peers were studying each other, and I felt an air of competition. I had a supercilious and almost cocky expression, but inside I fought the shaky, rattling nerves that were fixating me. I tried to do my best by appearing what perhaps was overly confident in order to help calm myself. What was scary for me was that all of the participants were really great. They were giving amazing and compelling speeches. These amazing speeches, which so much work was put into, were memorized with the highest levels of perfection. My turn was coming, and adrenaline started to rush through my blood.

The onstage presence within me started to ramp up like never before. All of a sudden, the infamous moment happened. My name was called. A microphone was connected to my black suit jacket, as I looked rather debonair for the event.

My palms started to get clammy, and the walk to the stage seemed endless. All eyes were on me, and this overwhelming sense of gut–wrenching, public fright emerged from nowhere.

The bright lights shined in the distance. The sheer volume of distractions clouded my memory. Within a split second, I forgot my speech. My body froze like I was a stiff Tin Man from *The Wizard of Oz* begging for oil to get me moving. I even felt like the famous Cowardly Lion, wondering what had happened to my courage.

It was clear from my nerve-racking sense of awkwardness that I had forgotten the speech, especially for those close to me who knew of the speech. My bosses, college professor, and family had that speech down like the back of their hands. After all, I had practiced it over and over to them as I prepared over the last few weeks. "How could this moment happen?" I asked myself.

Although the intensity could not have been more dramatic, I remember a crazy sense of unexplainable inner energy saving me. Out of the blue, the right words started to come to me. Suddenly, the speech came back to me, and I regained my confidence.

I focused on just telling a story rather than trying to give a speech. Suddenly, I began reconnecting the story to the audience.

It seemed that within moments the speech was over. Time had flown by as quickly as fingers snap.

The speech turned out great, and victory was mine. Yes, it was a miracle! Although I didn't win the competition, the effort alone was an accomplishment and growth experience that felt like a victory.

As I looked back at that event, it was amazing to feel that deep inner energy and belief overtake and prove my limiting belief wrong. I persevered and didn't cave in to the negative thoughts, and I am grateful for that opportunity.

Thinking about the scary thoughts of competition in running a race and giving a speech, I realized I can overcome limiting beliefs when I choose to. I realized that limiting beliefs are things we put on our own shoulders. We tend to carry negative thoughts on our shoulders like heavy backpacks.

When push comes to shove and we find ourselves in situations that test us and comfort zones that scare us, courage and perseverance are lifesavers! When we are doing something that has a deep-rooted purpose and we throw some passion behind it, successes come easier. The reason behind my speech was to inspire others. I was able to find that passion and connect it to the story. In my case, since the speech was erased for a moment, it would have been so easy to just throw in the towel and drop like a domino. The thought of walking off stage really came to me. However, giving up has never been an option. Being direct with fears and being bold enough to face them made me stronger.

No matter how hard the road gets, we always have the ability to persevere!

Because I pushed myself with public speaking, it helped me later on with my professional development. If we don't take risks because we are afraid to fail, then we never grow. In fact, in many ways we can hold ourselves back from what we are truly capable of achieving. In retrospect we can sell our own selves short.

David, a coworker I had several years ago, used to always give me great advice. One day, I listened as he spoke of opportunities. He was talking about how some people don't realize opportunity even when it is in front of their faces. He said, "Never sell yourself short when it comes to opportunities in life."

He was right. To this day, I always think about that. I use these thoughts today constantly, asking myself, "Am I selling myself short?"

A Speech to Be Remembered

During my speech that I gave in San Francisco, I tied a connection to a famous story of a racing horse named Zippy Chippy and its owner, Felix Monserrate. I had heard this story from someone in school, and it always stuck with me. It always inspired me!

Monserrate, whom I never had met, was someone I looked up to. Monserrate knew a thing or two about overcoming limiting beliefs, having steel courage, and persevering no matter what. Zippy Chippy is a New York-bred horse known as America's favorite thoroughbred racing loser. Many people would discourage Monserrate and tell him not to waste his time and energy prepping his horse. In fact, some people said that his horse had become a nuisance to horse racing.

Zippy Chippy had one of the worst racing records in history and was even banned at many events, where he was not able to race. People would get a comedy kick out of watching the horse because it was always so sloppy when competing. In spite of the pressure to give up, Monserrate still woke up every day and conditioned the horse. No matter what others said, no matter the outlook of failure, he gave it his all every day. Not once did Monserrate yield or cave in to the limiting belief that his horse wasn't good enough.

So why would Monserrate put himself through the ridicule and embarrassment all of this time? Why would he waste so much of his money knowing he would not achieve victory?

For Monserrate and his horse, who never made it to the winner's circle, the passion and love were triumphant. His love and passion for the horse were so stubborn that they molded themselves into resiliency. It wasn't about winning first place. It was about getting up every day, no matter what, and doing something just because he liked to do it.

It made him happy, and he thoroughly enjoyed it! He followed his passion.

In spite of how difficult this was for Monserrate, his story shows us the good we can truly accomplish by simply doing what we want to do, regardless of what others think or say.

It never mattered what others said or how they felt when it came to Monserrate following his passion and dreams. His story was able to help me realize that, regardless of how tough life gets, keep going. Persevere! Keep doing what you love to do, because it is what you love to do! It doesn't have to be about what someone else wants you to do!

Find something you love, and keep going!

CHAPTER 4
UNLIMITED BELIEFS

Limiting Beliefs

The limiting beliefs I have endured made me realize that instead of having a limiting belief in ourselves, we should really have *unlimited* belief in ourselves. The sky is not the limit unless you think it is!

Limiting beliefs do hit everyone in some way or another all of the time. In fact, they most likely hit us more than we realize.

Considering the challenges we face, life can sometimes feel like one enormous limiting belief. As we get older and the challenges become increasingly harder, we tend to push our own dreams aside—like a broom sweeping dust away.

People are constantly wondering if they are still capable and have the potential to achieve their dreams. Goals tend to get harder and harder to achieve. And in some cases, we die wondering what we could have done. For example, we oftentimes think of starting a new hobby, a new career, traveling somewhere, or doing something we always wanted to do. However, we become critical of ourselves and say, "One day," "I could have done that too," or "Now it is just too late."

Perhaps when we place these "someday" or "too late" limited beliefs on ourselves, they become *never*. "Sometimes" never transforms to regret. Every day is a beautiful opportunity to challenge, chase, and make an impact on moving the mountains in our lives.

Limiting beliefs are a part of our daily lives. When I think of limiting beliefs, I think of negative thoughts. They seem to be reminiscent thoughts that have likely been with us since we were brand new in the world. Until the day we die, they may stay with us. Limiting beliefs always seem to creep up in our rearview mirrors like the flashing lights of a police car, pulling us over and bringing us to a dead stop. Limiting beliefs ticket us and often make us fearful of them. What matters is how we control that negative thinking by activating our positivism deep inside.

Finding We Matter

As I continue to grow and see how I have fought adversity, I remember why I am worthy. We have to believe we are worthy in every life situation. I heard someone once say that we matter simply because we are who we are!

We are breathing, *living*, and full of hopes, dreams, goals, feelings, emotions, and, most importantly, beating hearts! The beating pulses every single day give us all the capacity we need to change so much in this world. The beat pounds every day, nonstop, so that each of us can make an unparalleled difference in this world. I strongly believe this!

Realizing Unlimited Beliefs

The truth is we can have and do whatever we want. The trigger is we have to want something badly enough and believe that anything can be possible. I believe that in our souls we all really do have unlimited beliefs, if only we push the limiting beliefs aside.

We all are geared with the right power to soar through the turbulence of limiting beliefs, if only we spread our wings of inner belief. I have reflected a lot in my life on how limiting beliefs can hold me back if I choose to let them. Many of the limiting beliefs that I have endured I have been able to overturn by digging deep.

An author named Christian D. Larson points out (in one of my favorite quotes): "Believe in yourself and all that you are. Know that there is something inside you that is greater than any obstacle."

Another one of my favorite quotes that reminds me of possibilities is from Audrey Hepburn, who said, "Nothing is impossible; the word itself says, 'I'm possible.'"

The invading force of negative thinking oftentimes concocts a limited belief factor. Negative thinking is what we become accustomed to feeling. It tells our inner selves that we don't deserve to have what we want. A literal negative factor is the prime thief that robs the very joy deep inside. The inner belief really starts the moment we think of ourselves in a positive way.

Thinking of Myself in a Positive Way

I was able to start thinking of myself in a positive way when I started to do positive things, such as volunteering in a nursing home. I would always reflect on something positive about my day. I was forming so many positive relationships that I could not help but to have a positive outlook on my life, myself and my future.

As I have weathered through enormous life challenges, I realized that no matter how challenging things are, someone else out there is in more troubled waters, struggling to stay afloat.

I have understood from the start that this world is full of tragedy and sad misfortunes. Hurt and pain are everywhere we look; we see it every day that we turn on the news or pick up a paper.

Considering the profound fact that many people in this world still die from hunger, disease, and cancer, we can see that we live in a world full of sadness. Many families are separated by losing loved ones, and some have no clue where they will sleep tonight and tomorrow night.

David Pelzer

I was reminded that even though my physical abuse was painful, it never compared to the type of abuse that others have gone through. I found a hero in 1998 after getting my hands on *A Child Called It,* a book written by David Pelzer. I read how David survived severe child abuse. His story hit home to me. I saw that David had it way worse than I ever did. Yes, there were different situations, but I still have a common appreciation for the strength David had as he survived. He literally, courageously, and miraculously survived. David is a hero to me for his strength. He served as a symbol of hope for me that recovery is possible.

The child-abuse cases are truly sad. It is so important to continue the campaign for awareness of child abuse. Now the Child Protective Services is an organization that does a great job helping abused kids. There is still a lot of work to do in order to help protect kids. Continuing the campaign for awareness is important because, unless abuse is reported, kids will continue to suffer.

The sad truth is that with all of the abuse out in this crazy world, many people will still never rise above those situations. Because of a limiting belief and fear, it is incredibly hard to find the courage to get out of bad situations. I have found that by being positive, we truly can have and should have unlimited beliefs for our lives and for our goals.

CHAPTER 5
COMING OUT

Coming to Terms

Coming to terms with being gay was not the easiest thing to do. All my life I have heard people make antigay comments. I would see constantly on the news gays fighting for equality and equal rights. As a matter of fact, today, whenever we turn on the television, we constantly hear about gay issues all over the place.

Knowing deep inside that I was, in a sense, a minority being, one of them, was very intimidating. No one knew of it other than me. Right now, there are still too many teenagers struggling with their sexuality. Gay teens face a huge amount of pressure and overwhelming challenges. They face the pressure that society imposes on them as they are realizing their identities. In all likelihood many of these same youth are establishing emotional intimacy with others for the first time.

The prejudices and bullying of gay, lesbian, transgender, and questioning youth are heartbreaking. I knew that being one of them would be a process for me for sure. I was afraid of rejection from not only my family and close friends but also the world. I thought of questions like these: How will people treat me if they find out, and will this mean that God hates me? These are serious questions that not only I struggled with, but many people still struggle with them every single day.

Matthew Shepard

In 1998, a year before I graduated from high school the grim and sad details of a young man named Matthew Shepard were on the minds of many. He was a bright teenager who was brutally murdered in an act of hatred and discrimination just because he was gay.

Shepard's death reminded me just how much hate is truly out there against the gay community. While hearing this story, it further frightened me to talk about my homosexuality with anyone. This story impacted many people, and many people will never forget. Nor should they forget this story.

The loss of Matthew had a profound impact on every single gay, lesbian, and transgender person across this nation. It also had a profound impact on heterosexuals as they realized the magnitude of the hate out there. Everyone typically knows someone who is gay. It is so sad to see such discrimination in our society—even today with how far we have come. We are reminded constantly that the fight for equality continues.

The Matthew Shepard Foundation is a wonderful organization that today helps people embrace diversity and human dignity. The foundation continues to be a live voice and leading voice in the gay community, and it does an incredible job raising awareness, resources, and support.

In my tough reality, I proudly stood for who I am in many circumstances. I had sought out resources, networks, and mentors who have helped guide me. I made bold steps, and it took a lot of courage for me to do so, but I admit I was scared. Although I was nervous, I did it anyway! I did face the limiting belief head on, even though it wasn't easy. After doing some research, I discovered some resources. Although I was scared to attend any gay group in general, I got in my car and buckled up anyway.

Thoughts surfaced regarding whether I was really strong enough to get help multiple times. The whole way across the Vallejo-Benicia Bridge on my way to Concord, these thoughts surfaced.

Support and Safety Zones

I showed up at The Community Center. I wasn't sure what to expect. When I walked in, I realized that people were around the same age as me. There were about a dozen people, including a counselor. They had a pool table and games. People were just talking and having a good time.

The environment was friendly, open, and warm. I was shocked to see that I wasn't alone and—wow—people my age were struggling too. This was a relief. I felt as if I would not be judged and it was okay to talk about my feelings.

Soon I started to look forward to going. When I turned nineteen, I started to go every week when I had free time. At this center I met friends and established a wonderful support system. This support system helped guide me through some tough terrain.

When I first started going to this center, I had no friends who were gay. I was scared to tell others who I was, and for the most part I was hiding my identity from the world as I tried to protect myself. But I finally felt as if I had a safe zone where I could relate and not be judged.

Many of these teens had been raised by strict religious families who despised or judged gays. Some of the teens didn't really have any parents, and some had parents but their parents had many of their own issues.

One person in particular who I will never forget was there every time I was there. His name was David. He was always very sheltered, reserved, and scared. I remember meeting him and seeing how timid he was. He just looked scared and hurt, and he really strived to get a support system going.

David was always afraid to talk to his parents about being gay. Like me, David went through physical violence, as he was beat up constantly. After seeing people like David, I realized that coping would be devastating without these support systems and community centers.

It was really sad to see how frightened he was of his own family. He was going through such pain alone and his parents had no clue. But this is the reality in the gay world, and too many people have to struggle with it. I could not fathom that a parent who loves his or her children would ever want them to feel so helpless and scared. Worse yet, I could not fathom that parents would want their kids to have to go through this horror and not want to be there for them.

Then again, I can't fathom that parents would ever want to hurt their kids physically or emotionally. Although no one is perfect and people make mistakes, even parents, it's a scary world.

Kids don't come with instruction manuals either. Although I am not a parent, I can see that parenting is no easy task. Regardless, I believe that parents should always create a safe zone for their kids, no matter what. Let's face it. We live in a crazy world full of issues that minors struggle with. Being gay is just one of these issues. Minors struggle with bullying, drug usage, and peer pressure, which are huge issues in our school systems. Now more than ever, the challenges youth face are significant. Every day we hear of budget cuts and programs like music, art, and sports being eliminated. The very things that keep youths going seem to be dwindling away.

Adolescents need to talk to their parents and feel safe in doing so. Parents need to be more involved than ever with the cuts to these vital resources and support networks and help with the realities of life. Parents and kids need to talk and connect on different levels. Parents have to create an environment in which their kids feel safe enough to talk about their struggles. Youths must feel safe, that it is okay to tell their parents anything.

I would think that all parents would want that special bond with their kids. Yet parents get blinded and assume that everything is okay. Parents will often ignore struggles their kids are having because some parents don't know how to help, give advice, or deal with certain situations. Hopefully, we can all agree that all adolescents need support and safe zones.

I would think that all parents love their kids wholeheartedly. No matter the issue, kids should always feel safe bringing their struggles to at least one of their parents. When they don't feel safe, oftentimes kids resort to giving in to those pressures and go down wrong paths. I have seen this happen plenty of times. I've seen it plenty of times to people very close to me. I had countless opportunities to go down those paths as well.

No matter what, parents and guardians should want to walk to the end of the earth for their kids. No judgments, no blaming, no making them feel less of a person, but just to listen, support, and love.

I know of many parents who have such a good relationship with their kids that they can talk about anything. They are more than parents to their kids. They are their best friends. They are the heroes in their kids' lives.

I would think that most parents would want to be heroes to their children.

None of my peers, family, or friends ever knew I went to this support center to find help on my own. I was scared of this since my family had gone through so much with all of the past violence. Many years passed by and I kept it quiet. Many years pass by for so many. I am meeting friends who are in their fifties and still are keeping it quiet from their families. It is like standing behind a strong, tall tree. The tree is a safe zone. Every now and then, you have the urge to peak out and tell someone, but they are just not sure how safe it really is.

Although I knew of my personal strength fighting the adversity, coming out was one of the hardest things to face. Realizing the fact I had nothing to be shameful of, nothing to hide, and I should be proud of who I am. It absolutely breaks my heart to know many people just like me face that adversity every single day.

From Adversity to Opportunity

Many don't know how to reach out for help. Facing that adversity alone is a recipe for so many painful struggles and more time that just passes.

While being faced with a limiting belief of fighting adversity with being gay, I looked to turn my adversity into opportunity. Mentoring others who faced the same adversity I faced is what I did. I had no professional skills, but I was able to connect and listen.

Quickly I realized that when helping others, you don't need to be a professional. You just have to be you. It also gave me strength, confidence, and the grace of knowing that I am worthy to be who I am and worthy to live the life I want to live. This thought gave me the sense of freedom, which I embraced.

While having the support structure that I had, I learned that everyone is different, with different personalities. I learned to appreciate people for who they are. I learned to appreciate even the ones I disagreed with. I also learned that no one ever likes to be judged by others. Although we are all different, we have the common struggles. We all want to be loved. We all want from others validation that we matter.

Among the imperfections we all have as humans, no one should ever have to apologize for who he or she is. The greatest words of wisdom I can offer to anyone who is struggling with sexuality are to face the limiting beliefs head on. You are worthy, you matter because you are who you are, and that is a beautiful thing.

No one else is you.

One of my favorite quotes, and I do have lots of them, is from Dr. Seuss, who knew a thing or two about appreciating people for who they are. He wrote, "Be who you are and say what you feel, because those who mind don't matter and those who matter don't mind."

I realized that creating safe zones on my own and taking advantage of all the awesome resources and organizations was such an imperative part of coming to terms with my sexuality. We just can't get through personal struggles by dealing with them by ourselves, hoping or ignoring they will go away. Most importantly, we don't deserve to deal with struggles alone. The biggest thing for me was I could not deal with this alone because I knew of my self-worth. I deserved to live my life and be happy!

I am so happy about the It Gets Better Project. The project was created to show hope to those who have lost hope and are contemplating suicide. It shows struggling youth the different level of potential and happiness they can have.

I am also happy to see the campaign, which says gays are not second-class citizens and should not be treated as such.

It is so important for all of us to realize that we can make such a difference for each other. We all can do a better job in recognizing and validating each other. When we see others going through problems, we need to lend a listening ear or a shoulder to cry on, or even to let a person know that he or she matters!

Help is everywhere out there; we just have to have the courage to get it. Volunteers stand ready. I can't stress enough finding that courage to pick up a phone, call a friend, or find a resource. The decisions we must make will never be easy. However, nothing is really ever easy when it comes to life choices and initiating getting help.

At the end of the day, we have to be responsible for our own selves. It is our life and no one else's life. This includes being happy for ourselves and what we are! We are responsible for our own happiness, the joys in our lives, the failures, and the successes.

I realized as I started to live my life after the years of abuse that not only was I finding myself, but I was also creating the life I was meant to live. It comes to standing up to the limiting beliefs that we automatically give constant fuel to. It means being self-aware, realizing we have to be our own advocates, thinking positive, and turning adversity into opportunity!

There are many roads we can go down in life. For the most part, we choose which road to go down. When we are unsure which one is right, we question, "What if?" The beauty of life is that there is no way to know what each road will bring. Sometimes, we just have to go on the road and realize that if it doesn't look like the right road, it is never too late to turn around and go down a different road!

Journals

Starting in early 2001, I began writing journal entries, which really meshed with my love for writing. It also helped me sort feelings out on paper. Writing became a great outlet for me and helped me discover so much more about myself.

The day was August 15, 2002, when Elaine and I went into a Barnes & Noble bookstore in Fairfield, California. We agreed we would write journal entries, and I continue to do them even to this day. Some entries, I would be very specific with events, and other days I would dig deep with feelings and thoughts. Most entries were brief, but others were long.

The purpose of the journal was clear from the first day I started my entries. In fact, I even gave my entries the title from a quote that still inspires me: "We don't remember days, we remember moments." The author is Cesare Pavese.

My whole life, I knew that I was gay. But I was so busy with life and its distractions that I avoided the subject because it was uncomfortable thinking about it. I didn't feel as if I had a safety zone at home to talk about my feelings. I created those safety zones—of course outside home.

Here are samples of some of the thoughts I was going through during the years:

09/05/2001
In addition to my time helping others at the community center, I found another resource. After networking, I was introduced to a guy who loved helping others. He is a gay professional who is pretty well known in the

college community. He hosts a weekly gay networking event at his place every Sunday night. It is open to pretty much anyone who would like to attend.

It is a great support network. At this event, guys my age would socialize, watch movies, and talk about random issues.

I was so scared about going for the first time but just decided to go. I almost didn't go tonight. Similar to the gay community center in Concord, I just went and it turned out to be great. I was introduced to some pretty cool people my age, and several of them are in the same boat as I am in. Most of these guys have jobs, they are my age, positive, and I can see myself becoming good friends with many of them.

I sure have taken some amazing steps this past week. I told my mom I was gay, and it went over easier than I expected. What a weight off my shoulders. She wasn't surprised. She said in her heart that she already knew. I told her about my partner, and she was excited. The truth is I am now very comfortable with the acknowledgment that I am gay.

Why would I want to continue to hide who I am and live a double life? I would say that over the last six months I have matured a lot. I am so glad my mom and my sister Elaine know. I feel liberated!

I even told my Realtor!

My Realtor walked into my condo and saw a dozen roses. She asked, "Who got you those?" Normally, I would have brushed this off and lied about it.

Not this time!

I told her they were from my partner. She said, "Cool!" She was excited to meet my partner, which was nice. It should never matter to someone else who we love.

01/05/2003

Today Elaine and I bonded as we sat at Starbucks in Hercules. After coffee, I went to her place in Crockett. That was a great salad she made. We talked for hours about goals, helping people, and, most interestingly, we talked about how having a great attitude is so important in life. She is right; it is all about attitude no matter the struggles, no matter the challenges that present themselves to us. If we have a good attitude, the outcomes will always turn out in a better way.

09/28/2005

Do your best! Have a sense of purpose. These are phrases I have put thought into during the last several days.

How many people wake up every day with these important thoughts? Really!

How many people wake up and say, "I will have a killer day and will do my absolute best?" Or how many people actually wake up and remind themselves of their purpose in life? *Hmmm.*

I guarantee that if a person wakes up with these thoughts in mind, then he or she would have a better attitude and do their best in everything.

Every day should be a day of purpose, spirit, and meaningful fun. Every day is intended for everyone in some special way.

11/02/2005

I just got back from the gym with my good friend Jeannine. It is a cold night and is about 9:30 p.m. A topic that stuck out to me this week was a conversation I had with a customer regarding a person's spirit. I thought about it and realized how our conversation ties in to my purpose.

If my spirit is always upbeat, motivating, and confident, that energy becomes inspiring to others.

When we are steadfast with our energy, that energy becomes who we are. People look for others who are inspiring, and this is a huge leadership trait that others tend to follow.

People react to spirit. Spirit is the fire-burning torch that carries people to believing in their strengths that maybe they never knew they had.

Tonight I am not going to let how someone feels bring my positive spirit down.

03/14/2006

Today John was released from the hospital. John, who is my partner's father, is in many ways my surrogate father. It is amazing how much support John has given to me in such a short amount of time. He has taken us to Disneyland and Vegas and spent all kinds of time with me. I think I will now be going to Disneyland a bit more often! Vacations were never this much fun for me. Experiencing a happy family vacation with no stress is amazing! John has shown me what it means to have fun. He has shown me love.

CHAPTER 6
MY HEALING PROCESS

What the Past Can Teach Us

No, I am not an expert at relationships. I don't have a
psychology degree. I am not a doctor of any kind, nor
am I an expert on healing. I can only talk about my own
healing process and how it has worked for me.

The healing process has been relieving, and I have
peace of mind knowing the past is the past. I came across
what would be my healing process in my early twenties. I
had been disregarding my negative past experiences and
focused on a positive lifestyle.

I realize many people unfortunately do live in the
past. A quote that always reminds of this is from Henry
Thoreau: "Never look back unless you are planning to go
that way."

I was happy for the most part. I definitely had full control over my life. That is what I had always wanted since I was young. Being positive is just who I am.

At this junction in my life, I didn't even really think of a healing process. After all, what really was there to heal from? A lot! However, I was so focused in on my career and supporting myself that I was overlooking those important questions.

I seemed to be fine. This is exactly what happens to a lot of people. They go through tough situations and just move on. Since they are not in the same bad situation anymore, people think they can just turn the page. People turn the page in relationships so quickly even in abusive relationships. The truth is everyone has to confront his or her past. Not to be confused with living in the past. Learning from the past and being able to identify feelings of the past that perhaps are hidden is so important.

Avoiding our past is like driving with a suspended license. You can keep driving, but eventually you will be pulled over and will need to face the reality. You must take care of things.

If we don't confront the past problems, they will resurface in the future in some way or another. This is a given. It happens. And, God forbid, we go down the road and become what we desperately tried to get away from, making sure we don't react to situations in the ways we don't want to. The past can haunt in many ways that bring significant consequences.

Our past has a lot to do with our future and who we are. I can see my past and pull the good from it to help create the future for myself. I can also sort out the negative and realize those are areas I will be mindful of but have learned from them. We will never forget our own history.

Once our past resurfaces, people can jump to the problems in their past to use as an excuse for their conduct, not taking responsibility and shifting blame on why they are who they are. Or why they did what they did. I have never been one to pull a "victim card" or "blame card." Instead, I tried to learn as much as I could from the situations I was in. I don't see my past as excuse for anything in my life other than to help people going through similar situations.

Taking Control

Since I had some major bumps in the road with childhood abuse, I realized it was my time to confront mine. Coming to terms with the torment I went through was a start. I started a healing process, which helped me to recover from the anger I still had deep inside. I realized this anger once I started to talk about it. I didn't always sense the anger in me, but I knew it was there. Pulling through this process helped further develop and fuel my inner belief even more. It would make me stronger and more confident about me. I learned that truly, in all issues that present themselves to us, we have to deal with them head on. Take the situations for what they are and not hide from them. We need to grasp the situation tightly, like holding on to handlebars. We can take control if we have the courage to ride what might seem a scary wave of hills.

Robert Frost provides wisdom into this: "The best way out is always through."

It is true; we have got to go right through any issue to get past it!

Although I did a great job overcoming a lot of negative with positive, not having a dad by my side still affected me—for that matter, he wasn't in my life after I turned eighteen and moved out of the house.

I started to read some books about others who had gone through very hard childhood abuses. It was important for me to read of others. I referred again to some of the Dave Pelzer books that I had read years ago. He had come out with more books. Again, his stories of survival helped me to discover what I needed to do in order to work, to turn the chapter.

I wanted to stand up to the past so I could give myself the gift of moving on. The problems earlier in life bleed through the crevasses of our happiness and hold us back. And, yes, oftentimes, when those haunting memories come back, if we don't deal with them then they start to steal our joy without us even realizing some of the effects. Sometimes, when we realize them, they may be too late.

Meeting Jim

As I started to really contemplate my healing process and read books from great authors, things started to fall into place. Suddenly, a great friend (a mentor) stepped into my life. It is so amazing how people weave into our lives at unique times. They enter the door when we need them the most.

At times, these relationships we form can be brief or they can be sustained. One evening, on September 5, 2002, I was invited to a friend's house for a party. I almost didn't go, as I was tired from a hard day of work. It was a normal house party. I didn't really know too many of the people there. However, I was trying to network and meet new friends. Out of nowhere, I saw an older person who saw me, and he started to make small talk with me.

Jim and I talked about all kinds of things in life. One would call this more of a profound conversation, but it just happened. Jim looked wise just because of the way he carried himself. Our chemistry immediately connected and, come to find out, he has counseled many people. He was also just steps away from previously becoming a Catholic priest.

His passion about being a Catholic stood out as something we had in common. I have always been deeply tied to my faith in God. And I believe it is that faith that has helped me be who I have always been naturally: a positive person.

Jim's priesthood training was put to use on me. We had an interesting dialogue and kept in touch very closely. After many conversations, he suddenly became such a strong mentor and friend in my life. Jim truly, from the start, made an impact on my early adulthood years. He helped me move along in the healing process. We started by first talking about it in depth. I hadn't done this for several years. Just merely talking about it, I began to acknowledge everything, and I just got it all out!

Accepting

I wrote down everything I remembered and truly expressed the misfortunes that actually happened to me. Jim helped me to accept the past abuse for what it was. He did this by connecting me closer to my faith than I had ever been before. Even though I had been an altar boy for ten years, gone to church every Sunday, and even attended church confirmation retreats, Jim helped me reconnect more strongly to faith than ever before. I was able to connect to that faith because I realized how that faith has helped transform me throughout the years.

Jim was there for me through thick and thin, and his support for me truly helped mature me. The fact that Jim walked into my life when he did was almost a miracle. Through the rest of 2002, Jim continued to coach me through my healing process.

In the healing process, I started a healing journal so I could keep track of my feelings. One of those days, I documented a conversation I had had with Jim regarding how I receive love. He said I was great at giving love to others. Then he asked, "But Michael, how do you give love to yourself?" He also asked, "How do you trust others?"

He was right on by saying that. I have dedicated my whole life to helping others. But how was I appreciating and loving myself? I was not really attuned to this. It opened a whole world of new discovery about me. I am so giving toward others. Jim triggered my self-awareness, which made me feel even more passionate about helping others. So I started to be more self-aware of my own feelings.

I started to keep close track of my thoughts and write extensively about the abuse I had gone through. Writing about the trust issues taught me more about the importance of boundaries in life.

As I started to realize and draw the connections of everything I had done to help others, I appreciated more about where I had been. I appreciated more about who I was and appreciated more about where I was going. It was gratifying and important to write about everything I had gone through, and it did help me come to terms. The experience was painful and dramatic, yet it was invigorating.

By my revisiting what happened and acknowledging I was able to get to the next point, which was confronting my father.

That courage I found in the healing process. It pushed me to want to get over the past and become stronger for it. That resiliency in me started to burst through yet again. And that thriving inner belief relit the candle, again which gave me the confidence to confront my father and be okay with it.

My brother, sisters, and I wrote a joint letter being specific about accounts of abuse and how those accounts made us individually feel.

He several weeks later responded back stating he was sorry. Years later, in 2010, my father resurfaced and apologized in person. I did let him know that I forgave him.

Forgiving my father was the greatest gift I gave to myself. The anger, hard emotions, and fear I let go. I did not want to keep living with anger in my blood. But forgiving doesn't mean that I have forgotten.

I have peace through forgiveness. Now I was able to turn the page and be at peace. Today, there isn't a relationship that exists between him and me.

I am comfortable that I came where I did in the healing process.

It was truly amazing that Jim helped me with this process the whole way through. Today Jim is still a very close friend, and mentor. I am very grateful to him.

In addition to Jim, as I went through my healing process I found other resources. Conversations with my mom, sisters, and brother were all very helpful in the healing process. Talking about those times really helped all of us to recover in our own ways. I leaned a lot on my other friends through the process. A healing process is never meant to be done alone. Personal coaches, counselors, and mentors are out there. The resources out there are unbelievable. There are incredible books that offer assistance around healing.

Looking at my bad memories in the eye and confronting them was the hardest part in my healing process. During this process, I became closer than ever with family. We all further connected to each other; everyone endures healing in their own internal ways.

With every hard time, somehow, by some unexplainable reason, a good time is created. The good time in this case was our family supporting each other in ways we had never done before. Hard times and good times bring families and people together. Those hard times though are different. In some families, hard times separate them. The will to weather through during the hard family times is the test for the strength of the family.

Regardless of what happens, we can control our reactions and how we handle our situations. By us simply having a great heart and being a part of the solution, we personally will overcome the experience no matter what.

Chapter 7
Heroes

A Friend Named Josh

When we think of people who have made a difference in our lives, oftentimes what we find are that the things that were done weren't big things at the time; they were small. These were moments that we will never forget. At the time, maybe they were what we thought were small moments. Now we look back and realize those small moments were huge moments.

That is what it has turned out to be for me. In the years after graduating from high school, I started to grow great friendships with people I looked up to. I didn't have a lot of best friends from school when I was growing up since I dedicated so much time to volunteering. There was one person though who became a huge influence to me. His name was Josh.

Our mutual positive thinking is what brought us together as close friends. We connected with our positive thinking. Josh taught me a few things on overcoming limiting beliefs from back in our track and cross-country days. He was so positive and helped me stay positive even when I wanted to give up and quit. We conditioned together since there weren't many dedicated distance runners on the track team. To help us be great in track, he asked me why Hogan High School didn't have a cross-country team. I told him because they had no coach, no money for the program, and no resources.

He helped me realize that none of that mattered and that I could create all of that if I wanted to. One thing can create everything; it is called leadership.

It was possible to get a cross-country team together if I was determined to make it happen. I convinced my English teacher to be the coach. Done. We had a coach! I sought out track friends, and suddenly there were a handful of us.

It took plenty of convincing, but we did it. Found the people—done! We had a team!

The uniforms we managed to get by working with the athletic director and convincing the school—done! Then we registered and were now able to compete with other teams.

Running cross-country is an extremely mental sport due to the longevity you must possess to muster through long runs and the wildest and hardest terrain. Getting ready for a meet means you not only have to condition yourself physically but mentally as well. During most running events, Josh and I usually stayed pretty close to each other. Oftentimes we led the pack of distance runners. We constantly pushed each other even during the hardest and most exhausting times.

Don't Stop

One day in particular was extremely hot, and I was tired. Josh saw me starting to slow down. He surely enough fell behind me and kept shouting, "Don't stop! Don't stop! Keep going, Mike."

Those simple words kept me going. The simple words and belief that others have in us are sometimes what it takes to push that fire energy deep inside ourselves to win.

Josh and I kept each other strong, and our friendship kept building. Tragically, on April 10, 2000, Josh was killed in a car accident. This was not long after our running seasons were over.

Never in a million years did I think I would be a speaker at my best friend's funeral. Dealing with his death was one of the hardest things for me to deal with. I will be forever grateful of the memories and moments. Such a positive person left us too soon.

His death tore the community of Vallejo's heart. To this day, I look back at the times we shared and the words he used: "Don't stop!"

Oddly enough, just a few months after his death I was reading a running magazine and a page caught my attention quick. It was an ad of a guy running past a stop sign. And, the sign said, "Don't Stop." The two words that had once pushed me pushed me again to never forget. I tore that page out of the magazine and still hold onto that picture today. I look at it frequently and live that motto: "Don't Stop!"

There are far too many stop signs in our lives. We would never achieve anything if we stopped at every stop sign. We see those stop signs and we keep barreling forward. That is not only what leads us to success; it leads us to a life we are capable of having. Thinking boldly, thinking big, and thinking better help me understand why it's so important that we *don't stop!*

Josh will always be a hero in my life.

Heroes in My Life

Several years ago, I had the opportunity to work for a manager who taught me a lot about leadership. One day she invited all of her managers to her house. She did a team-building exercise by asking each manager to write down the names of our heroes. We were to write down all of the one-word adjectives that described this person in one minute and then share with our peers.

One person I immediately thought of quickly came to my head. I wrote down my sister Elaine. Here are the words I used to describe her: inspiring, survivor, strong, fighter, motivating, listener, integrity, courageous, caring, reliable, trustworthy, uplifting moments, and true.

Once we wrote down all of the words all of our peers shared by reading the one word adjectives they came up with. Soon it was my turn to read off all of the one word adjectives. I proudly did so. I folded the piece of paper and kept it. Saying all those words and not just writing them down really made me feel proud of my sister.

My sister Elaine is someone who has always believed she can do anything. After a grueling, abusive, and painful childhood, she put herself through college. She was the first to go through college. She did it without any resources. There was a lack of encouragement from others for her to go to college. Encouraging herself was the biggest encouragement out there. She was her own and only resource at the time. I saw how hard she worked and how tirelessly she endured the pain of not having a relationship with her family through many years.

The biggest support she had included friendships, hope, and pride. It was the everyday type of friend that gave words of encouragement and a shoulder to cry on.

Her eyes were always focused on the goal she had set for herself, which was to graduate from the University of California at Davis. The confidence and hope she had in her heart showed a spirit that was bulletproof.

One day Elaine managed to sneak around and pick me up from the house. My father, after all, for several years had not allowed her over to the house and blocked the relationship I had with Elaine. She drove me to Davis for the first time. She had picked me up in her red Tercel that she counted on.

During the ride up, she showed me where she worked, and then she toured the beautiful campus.

Soon, it was time for lunch, and I remember seeing her struggle to find food. She had managed to make sandwiches back at her apartment. We took the sandwiches and went to a park on campus. I took a few bites and was not going to finish it. She started to cry when she saw I wasn't going to finish it. She said, "Michael, please eat the sandwich and not waste it."

Then it clicked. I saw how much she was struggling and how hard she was fighting to create a better life. She had little money, and I saw the pain of what she was going through.

I will never forget this time and how hard she was working to achieve her dreams. Elaine worked several part-time jobs that paid low wages. Elaine was in the midst of the pursuit of her own happiness, and she worked tirelessly. She suffered the added stress of knowing her little brothers were at home living with many struggles. This was a constant nightmare for her.

Figuring out how she would come up with money every month continued to be a struggle. Her will to overcome limiting beliefs and support herself is what I have always admired. She showed relentless strength. Elaine has always been a fighter. During her college graduation, overwhelmed by the sea of cheers, I was so proud. This was the first time I ever went to a college graduation. Beating all odds, she did it!

Soon after college, Elaine decided to become a firefighter. This was hard for her since she was, after all, a female entering a very conservative, male-dominated profession. She constantly dealt with battling a limiting belief that tried to convince her to do something else. Being an integral part of a firehouse was a bit controversial and every day she had to be strong. Her passion truly guided her to follow through on her dream.

Elaine just didn't decide to be strong. She *stayed* strong. She had to continue getting up every day and face her challenges head on. Every day is a new day. Every day is a different challenge, and every day is a fight to have what you want in life. Every day, someone can take it from you if you let him or her, and every day we can give in to ourselves and quit. Yet every day we must motivate our self. We must stand up for who we are and what we want!

The dream to be a firefighter was inherited from our grandfather, who was a high-ranking fireman in Connecticut. Elaine stood up to the test of the challenges and now looks back with no regrets. Personally for her, the learning and growth experience from it was incredible.

Our grandfather would be so proud.

It was inspiring to many of her friends, and along the way she transformed the thinking within the fire department. She made a difference. They saw her determination and daily mental motivation. They saw that she never wavered from her passion and goals. The firehouse became so close to Elaine.

Many people go through these similar situations and, in spite of the challenges, rise up to be stronger than before. The toughest times that we unfairly experience as humans help to cultivate the best in us. They are moments that define us.

There were other heroes who came along to help pull me through to a strong pathway. I looked up to many of my previous managers, teachers, and coaches. I saw leadership in them all. I wanted to model myself after each of them.

We all have of course famous heroes. One of mine has always been Michael Jordan. Not only is he an athletic symbol and legend, he has an inspiring personal story. In Michael Jordan's career, he makes no apologies for failing. He missed more than nine thousand basketball shots, and he lost three hundred games. He was trusted twenty-six times to take the game-winning shot and missed. He said in a commercial, "This is why I succeed."

Jordan teaches us all not to fear failure but to embrace it. We can't make excuses in life. He also teaches that one thing that is more important in life than courage is patience. It is easy to lose patience and give up.

Staying determined, steadfast, patient, and focused, hard work will begin to pay off.

Along the way, I have always admired people in our time and in our history who have achieved great things against odds. Two who stand out, and whom I love reading about, are Abraham Lincoln and Martin Luther King Jr.

I could go on and on writing about famous people I look up to.

I believe that the most powerful thing about a hero is how he or she can influence you in later years of your life. Sometimes, you never forget what heroes teach you. Yet they have no clue at the time they are making such a great impact on you and what you may become.

One person who fit that description was a simple person named Bill. Every Sunday, he attended the same church I attended. Bill was in charge of the altar boys so he would oversee as I prepared for another Mass. Although my interactions with Bill were always very brief, I saw him every single Sunday for ten years. Bill was a former marine, and he taught me more than he ever knew. He always was on time, he was dependable, his tie was tied impeccably every time, and he was always positive. So even though I saw him briefly at church every Sunday, he made an impact on my life. He never realized I looked up to him or that he was a hero to me.

Today, I am still always doing things that he taught me. For example, others can depend on me, I try to dress the part always, and I believe in the goodness of doing quality work.

Bill taught me how to tie a tie the right way.

Before he died suddenly, he had some incredible conversations about my potential in life. He in many ways was a dad figure to me when I was so young. It's interesting how certain moments stick with us throughout the years. The moments are the ones that shape our lives.

I believe that every person on this planet is a hero to someone. Sometimes, the simple words of encouragement, continuously from a person, go further than we may know.

The power of mentorship is so profound. Mentorships create a lifelong impact on us. And they help to create who we are and where we are going in life. In many ways, mentors are heroes.

Some people consider themselves to have a personal life coach. I have had the pleasure of working with someone who fits that description very well in my life. His name is Glen, and he worked with me for several years. He helped hold me accountable to goals that I created for myself. He directed me and redirected me when I was off pace. Glen knows me.

I always set the agenda with our conversations, and it is amazing how much I grew from a simple one-hour talk. I would highly recommend that everyone has this type of relationship. These are people who help ground us and keep introducing us to new horizons!

In many ways, these types of people help to develop more of what we are capable of achieving in life. In life, we always have our greatest peaks when mentors are coaching us.

The gift of mentoring is truly a gift that we give every day and may not even realize it! We have a lot of people around us who can help tune us up. We hear about people who can tune us up. Yet we have to drive those miles to get to our destination.

Mentoring Others

It wasn't until I entered high school that school and grades became a priority for me. Instead of making everyone else happy, I knew I had to work on me. School needed to be a greater focus.

Track and cross-country, of course, were priorities. I discovered that I loved mentoring others. I stepped up to the plate and took on many leadership projects. I was introduced to an organization called Friday Night Live, which I still have a lot of passion for. Friday Night Live (FNL), also known as Club Live, is an organization that raises awareness on alcohol and drug prevention. It is a program that develops friends to be mentors to one another. Many schools have similar organizations.

Like inspiring patients in a nursing home, this was my chance to inspire hope in people my own age who struggled in different ways. I participated in leadership positions within the FNL community, which helped make a difference in many lives.

In addition to my involvement with FNL and running, I began working for the school newspaper. And I even started working for the city newspaper, the *Vallejo Times Herald*.

I loaded myself with positivity and busy events. I kept expanding myself to the good things in life. I stayed away from the negativity of home life and looked everywhere for brighter opportunities. For a time, I became more interested in politics. I heard of a program that allowed high school students to go to Washington, DC, to meet important political figures. Through the grapevine, others were talking of the program at my school. It was a limiting belief that made me think that I was not good enough to get into the program.

Coach Hicks

I had a lot of respect for Coach Hicks, who was also one of my teachers. And he was a part of the Vallejo city council. Coach Hicks really taught me that anything is possible but that you must work hard to get what you want.

He had known I had a passion for leadership and had nominated me to attend the National Young Leaders Conference (NYLC) in Washington, DC. I was given the green light, and I was so excited! I attended the conference in February 1999 and became an alumnus representing the organization.

It was a great experience. I was able to get a ticket to sit on the floor of the House of Representatives. During this time, President Clinton's impeachment trials were happening.

I met Senator Diane Feinstein and was able to have a one-on-one meeting with Congressman George Miller. Both of them represent California. During our conversations, we talked about issues affecting my school. And we had talked a lot about the FNL cause.

I can't forget that meeting since I had laryngitis and it was incredibly hard for me to talk. I was a bit embarrassed, but the interaction was amazing!

During that experience I was able to meet several members of Congress and interact with my local state leaders in Washington. The NYLC still exists today and is an incredible program with fascinating opportunities for those who have a passion for government.

I have always been interested and in tune with political issues. Coach Hicks never realized the impact he made on my life by sending me to this incredible event. After coming back from it, and still today, I have a greater respect for how our democracy works. So now I am more attuned to and passionate with what is happening in the political arena.

Having the opportunity to participate in these events showed me a new side to life. There are huge opportunities out there! Needless to say, with all of the extracurricular activities I was doing, I was not at home very much! Instead, I was busy focusing on positive things. I was having a great time. This is how I controlled having a good life.

Coach Lapid

I will never forget how my track and cross-country coach inspired me. To this day, I remember things she said to me. Coach Lapid would always pull the team together and tell us, "In running and in life, always just do your personal best."

To this day, I still remember those words, which always resound in my mind when I face great struggles or challenges.

Running and competing became a great outlet for me to deal with the stress of home life. Being able to win track events and succeed in long-distance events helped me to overcome limiting beliefs. I never imagined I would be good with running in competitions.

Once I had the courage to make those steps, there were mentors who helped carry me through to greatness. Coach Lapid helped me realize it is okay to take risks. Just do it! It's the same feeling we get just before we jump in a pool. Once we jump in and suck it up, the chills aren't as bad as we thought they would be. Once we jump in, we realize it was worth it.

We can only live our life once, so we might as well experience the thrill of jumping in! Jump into new things, even when you're unsure!

In addition to running track, I started to work at my first real job, which was at McDonald's. I pulled away from volunteering since I was busy with the focus on high school and work. McDonald's taught me a lot about teamwork and helped me develop natural people skills.

I quickly became a manager at McDonald's and loved being able to make a positive influence on the people I worked with. At this time, I also worked for the local newspaper. Literally, I had no time to absorb myself with the negative consequences of being at home. Having the responsibilities with a part-time job also boosted my self-confidence.

I started to realize I could take charge of my life. And so that is exactly what I did. I really started to overcome the fear of the abuse I suffered through.

I was in many ways trying to become self-sufficient so I wouldn't need to count on my parents to take care of me.

Overcoming the fear that sometimes plagues our lives is one of the biggest gifts one can give to oneself. Mothers and fathers always wish for their kids to be happy in life. I can honestly say the same standard is true for kids to their parents. All kids want their parents to be happy.

During my high school years, I sure did grow and learn a lot with all of the positive, busy experiences I went through. Closing the chapter of abuse was such an important step for me.

The positive relationships I formed and the hope they gave helped teach me I can have whatever I want. I can create what I want in my life, and in a sense I hold the pieces to my puzzle. It is truly up to me to put it together.

I moved into my own place when I turned twenty and focused on developing my banking and college career. Being out on my own helped me really develop my independence. It also introduced me to meeting incredible new friends who totally changed my life.

As I started Heald College of Business and juggled work full time, I learned so much so quickly. I confronted limiting beliefs very often, as I was tired from all of the juggling I did. When confronted with the stampede of daily life and the fatigue, I looked to what would be the reward, the final outcome.

Working truly hard for everything was special to me. And until now, I know we have to work hard for what we want.

I quickly made the dean's list several times and started to get serious about school for the first time. I had some very memorable college professors. One really pushed my writing skills and another pushed me in general—and still to this day pushes me.

The professors kept me inspired during the time I worked late hours and stayed in class to 10:30 p.m. I centered myself around positive people, which helped me succeed during those long days.

While I attended, I met so many professionals looking to advance their lives by getting a higher education. It was inspiring to hear their stories of trying to make ends meet as they were attending school, working full-time jobs, and being parents. In this light, I saw others working toward overcoming limiting beliefs and also realized that no one ever gets it easy. We are all trying to make ends meet in some way or another.

During this year, I had a talk with one of the bank executives who I really didn't know too well. I didn't think he knew me well either. I received an invitation to his office where we had a one-on-one meeting. He reminded me that others had a lot of stock in me. And I will never forget that conversation. I asked him what he meant by that exactly. He said, "Keep your goals high. Others look up to you more than you know."

For me, who says everyone is a mentor in some way, it hit that even I am a mentor in some way to others. It is a great feeling to know that everything we do has influence on others.

Keeping a simple, positive attitude can lift a day like glimpsing a rainbow after a storm. One sudden moment can turn the face of one's day.

We may not always have the power to change people. Yet we do have the ultimate power to influence others by being positive. And we can turn limited beliefs to inner beliefs, if we have the confidence to believe in ourselves.

With everywhere we go in life—work, school, meetings, gym—we truly choose to go to that place every day. We can choose to be happy.

We all have experienced being in a depressing meeting where everyone is complaining. We have all been in a work environment that people aren't happy in. When we find ourselves in those situations, we have to be the leaders and make them positive no matter how negative the environment may be. Being the leader is even more important if it is in a career we are dedicating ourselves to. We always have to be a part of the solution in anything in life.

CHAPTER 8
LIVING POSITIVITY

Conditioning Positivity, Living Positivity

It is amazing what happens when we are living positivity. But trying to be positive and living it are two different things. By conditioning ourselves to be positive, we become more positive. I think of working out, for example. It takes time to get the look we want. We have to condition ourselves and change our eating habits. In time, we become fit.

I believe the same is true for positivity. We don't just decide to be positive. We have to condition ourselves to be positive.

One evening a few years ago, my friends and I went to a nice restaurant in downtown Reno, Nevada. The restaurant overlooked the Truckee River and was well known. It wasn't the cheapest restaurant in town. It was pricey.

My friends and I were laughing together and enjoying the nice jazz music. I could not help but notice a lady sitting all by herself in the corner, where she was enjoying a nice meal. She seemed to be having a good time, as she was bopping her head to the tunes. She was dressed nicely for the occasion. I talked about my findings to my friends, and we decided to surprise her by picking up her tab. The lady was shocked to find out that we took care of her bill.

She thanked us, and we came over and talked to her for a bit. It turns out she was in Reno for a conference and was just checking things out. We made her night worthwhile.

She made me happy because I know she probably overcame a limiting belief by dressing up and treating herself to a nice, expensive restaurant. The lady was comfortable enough in her skin to not just sit in a hotel room and feel sorry for herself. She could have gone to a cheap restaurant, but no. She wanted to have a good time. Even though she was by herself, she didn't use that as an excuse not to have a good time.

This is what I am talking about. Do it anyway! This is an example of what happens when you are living positivity. My whole life, I learned that the best way to create positivity is to do positive things. It is the little things. Maybe it is paying for a person's coffee at the drive-through. Or maybe it is just talking with and encouraging a friend.

Positive people see other positive people, and they gravitate toward each other. More positive experiences happen when we are naturally positively fit!

No one can make you happy but you. Others can certainly help the process, but we are happiest when we activate that force within ourselves first.

Every single day among all of the life choices, no matter how little they may appear to be, we make our day a happy day or a sad day.

What has worked really well for me is that I keep exploring new challenging goals, new heights, and new adventures. Many who know me would call me a risk taker. We have to continuously reinvent goals. I love setting tough goals and working hard to achieve them.

Vision Boards

One of my favorite life coaches I love to follow is Jack Canfield. He once mentioned, "Your vision is a detailed description of where you want to get to. It describes in detail what your destination looks like and feels like."

For the last two years, I have had a vision board. The idea came from a family friend named Lisa. She is one of the most positive people I know. Lisa gets together with a group of friends once a week, and they talk about various issues. They help each other and offer advice to each other.

One of the activities they do is hold each other accountable for their vision boards. So I thought it was a great idea and started my own vision board. I went through magazines and cut out pictures of what I wanted to achieve in my life for that year. For example, I cut out a picture of a plane, representing that I would travel a lot during the year. I cut out a runner, because running was something I wanted to get back into.

I hung the vision board next to my closet so I would see it every single day. What is on this board is our vision for our goals and life. I had on it the word *inspire*. This way, I could remember every day to ensure I was inspiring people, so of course that was my purpose in life.

After seeing this board every day, I started to do everything on it. And I saw successes happen in my life. I was accomplishing my goals.

I presented the board to my sister Elaine. And she created her own vision board. Now we were able to hold each other accountable for goals.

I still do a vision board today. I also send out a quote of the day to several of my friends. Living positivity really means living positivity. The more positivity we create, the more positive experiences we have.

Stepping Out of Comfort Zones

When I was working in Concord at my banking job, I saw an opportunity and wanted it. The opportunity was in San Jose, which meant it was more than an hour from where I lived. It was two hours away, considering traffic.

I drove the distance for my interview. My nerves were shaky since I knew this was a career step, and the money would help since I was on my own. This was my chance to take a risk and step out of my comfort zone a bit. I pushed myself to the interview.

In moments where we are really striving for a better opportunity, limiting beliefs force us to question if we are really ready for the step. With my strong faith in overcoming the limiting belief, I blew away the interviewers and got the job.

I drove to work for the next year even though it was a two-hour commute every day.

Even among the crazy rat race of Bay Area traffic, the life-changing sacrifices I made helped transform my career in banking. I learned firsthand that opportunities are seldom labeled. When we see an opportunity we want, we have to have the courage to do it. Go for the final stretch and stretch the potential that lies within us.

I loved this new position. I felt like I was contributing and I was working with very positive people.

Had I never stepped out of my comfort zone and taken a risk, I never would have had that positive experience, which also led to a positive career experience.

While I started to work in San Jose, I made a three-year goal. One of the goals was to own a piece of property within three years. I actively pursued my goals. Within six months, I figured out how to do it, and I jumped on the opportunity.

I bought my first place when I turned twenty-one. For me, only being twenty-one was a major risk. The limiting belief was I could never make it and the drive was too far to do this by myself.

Making all of these moves was not always the easy thing to do. After all, I had to say good-bye to a lot of people who had helped develop me. Specific to my career in banking, I had formed amazing relationships. Saying good-bye to ones who helped support, develop, and mentor you is hard. As we move on to the new relationships, we always look back at what we had in our lives. When we reminisce about the people who influenced and changed us, we remember them as our heroes. After we have moved on and created more change, we meet more people who continue to change us.

By meeting more people, we go through different types of life situations that further define us. More friendships and alliances are formed. And along that way, we find our confidantes, friends who will always be with us no matter what we eventually move on to.

Sometimes we have to force ourselves out of our comfort zones—not fearing failure but embracing the exciting journey ahead.

Seeking the Right Friends

Our foundations are stronger than we sometimes give ourselves credit for. Perhaps we can't even fathom how strong our foundations really are until they are tested.

We are survivors in many ways with a surviving mentality. It is built into every bone that we have. Surviving instincts are in our blood as humans.

The close friends I have always sought are people I look up to. Life is full of choices, and making choices to hang out with people we don't look up to is one of the ingredients for trouble. If we center ourselves around negativity, and negative people. It can feel like an avalanche of problems coming towards us. It can bury as alive with burdens, tragedies and problems. It cascades into more problems and constant unnecessary stress, drama and unhappiness.

I have always had several people who were mentors to me. All of my friends were and still are mentors. I have to say, they are all my heroes.

I have a best friend whom I look up to with a great deal of respect. His name is Tony. Tony maintains life balance, has goals, and is constantly striving to get better. For more than ten years, Tony and I have been close, and I can always count on his support. No matter the circumstances, Tony looks to find the positive in any situation.

Who our friends are says a lot about who *we* are! Choosing to be with people who don't have goals or who are not looking to be better in life drags us down. I know of a few situations where I have seen some great balanced friends try changing others who weren't balanced. In most of those cases, the friendships eventually dwindled away.

Another important person in my life is a guy named Brandan. He is living proof that you can have anything you want if you stay focused and live a positive life. Brandan always had a vision of becoming a doctor. I met him just as he was finishing his undergraduate work. He worked really hard and made really hard decisions. When all of his friends wanted to go out, he sacrificed time to stay focused. Yet he lived a very balanced life.

Balance was important to Brandan. He was able to pull through because of the positive relationships he had with so many near him. Everyone helped rally him to stay focused and do well.

Sure enough he became a doctor, and all that hard work did pay off. I am extremely honored to be surrounded by such friends.

Living positivity is my life. No matter the adversity, if we stay positive we can do amazing things, be amazing things, and see amazing things.

It is amazing how many small or minor choices we make. More amazing is how often we try to hold others responsible for our own happiness. My greatest lesson in life has been that I am responsible for my own happiness. No one else controls that. This includes my doing things that make me happy, even when no one else is around. Like cooking, because I love to cook.

Living positivity is constant. It is constantly gratifying, and this is a gift I hope to give to anyone who reads this memoir.

Several years ago a friend named Dan was talking to me about how he sees life. What he said always stuck with me and it is also how I see life. He mentioned he sees life as a huge puzzle. Every day we are looking for the right pieces. Sometimes, we feel like we have found the right ones. And, when we think we have found those right pieces, we go to put them in only to find they don't fit.

We then try to force the pieces in anyway. But suddenly we realize it is time to look for another piece. Then we search some more, and we find it! Relief sets in at how easily it fits. We hope to have our puzzle done one day, but it does take some time to complete it. And once we have finished it, we start another.

Yes, our lives are big puzzles that are just as limiting as beliefs are. Sometimes, the puzzle is very hard to put together. And during life changes, we are forced to put together more and more puzzles.

So the beauty of life is staying positive and being open to experiences rather than fighting them once they have happened to us.

I stumbled over a quote by an author named Matthew Stasior, who said, "You must motivate yourself, *every day!*"

I have frequently gone back and reread that quote. It really reminds me to keep fighting.

Once we stay motivated, we create a habit of being motivated. Motivation starts with our individual selves. I truly live my life by this quote. If we wait for someone to motivate us every day of our lives, it can become challenging. We realize the hard reality that we have to chase our goals and dreams ourselves.

Always rely on yourself!

My Biggest Advocate

At the end of the day, throughout the struggles and pains I endured, my life was always up to me. I had to keep pressing forward. No one else could drive or motivate me every day.

In my youngest years, I was still always my own biggest advocate. I still had to endure. I had to be. We all have to be our own biggest advocates, no matter what, because it is our life and no one else's. We have to make the most of it and live the life we dreamed of living. No matter the challenges, no matter the pain, we have every opportunity to have the life we dream of.

I hope people who have gone through hard life struggles and then read this memoir can find their own positivity and live the life they wish to live.

> "The tragedy of life is not that it ends so soon, but that we wait so long to begin it."
> —W. M. Lewis, author